WEALTH AND THE POWER
OF WEALTH IN CLASSICAL ATHENS

WEALTH AND THE POWER
OF WEALTH IN CLASSICAL ATHENS

John K. Davies

THE AYER COMPANY

Salem, New Hampshire

Editorial Supervision: Steve Bedney

Reprint Edition 1984
AYER Company, Publishers, Inc.
47 Pelham Road
Salem, New Hampshire 03079

MONOGRAPHS IN CLASSICAL STUDIES
ISBN for complete set: 0-405-14025-8
See last pages of this volume for titles.

Manufactured in the United States of America

Library of Congress Cataloging in Publication Data

Davies, John Kenyon.
   Wealth and the power of wealth in classical
Athens.

   (Monographs in classical studies)
   Revision of pt. 1 of the author's thesis (Ph. D.
--Oxford, 1965) originally presented under title:
Athenian propertied families, 600-300 B.C.
   Bibliography: p.
   Includes indexes.
   1. Elite (Social sciences)--Greece--Athens--His-
tory. 2. Upper classes--Greece--Athens--History.
3. Wealth--Greece--Athens--History. 4. Athens
(Greece)--Genealogy. I. Title. II. Series.
HN650.5.Z9E43   305.5'2   80-2647

   ISBN 0-88143-019-6   AACR2

WEALTH AND THE POWER OF WEALTH

IN CLASSICAL ATHENS

by

J.K. DAVIES

Rathbone Professor of Ancient History and Classical Archaeology

University of Liverpool

CONTENTS

PREFACE

Δὶς κράμβη θάνατος, says the Greek proverb : 'warmed-up cabbage is death.'
I hope not. My original thesis of 1965 comprised three volumes, of which
volumes II and III were published as Athenian Propertied Families in 1971 with
minor amendments and with a brief introduction cannibalized from volume I. The
rest of volume I, apart from one section, has lain on my shelves largely
unused except as the basis of some of my Oxford lectures, to become a challenge
and an embarrassment as other commitments supervened. In consequence Professor
Connor's invitation to me to refurbish it for publication in this series came
as a timely and most welcome solution. I am very grateful to him and to the
Arno Press for their encouragement to revise and for their confidence that
the rechauffé still contains some wholesome fare.

I have made the following changes from the 1965 version. To prevent
confusion with APF, the book as here published is given a separate title.
References to source-material have been updated where necessary. Cross-references
have been made to refer to APF as published, with the convention that a number
double-underlined represents the bold numbers used in APF. References to
modern scholarship have been changed to conform with the Harvard system, and
in this and other ways the bulk of the original footnotes has been drastically
slimmed. In the hope that this book may be more accessible to the Greekless
than APF is, I have given translations for all the Greek quotations and words
which remain in the text. The section of the original thesis which became an
article in JHS 87 (1967) has been omitted. Also cut out has been some of the
material used for the Introduction of APF, but there does unavoidably remain
some repetition of material, amounting in all to a few pages. A few references
to post-1965 scholarship have been inserted, but only when a particular turn

in the argument could be directly followed up. After some hesitation I have retained Appendix I, mainly in order to redeem the promise made in APF p. xxvi to explain my interpretation of the diadikasia-documents. I am now aware that there is much more to say about these documents, and hope to publish further thoughts on them in due course, but it now seems to be essential to make an interim argument available for discussion. Appendix II has been up-dated to provide what purports to be a complete, 1980-based list of known military officials between 500 and 300 B.C.

Even taken together, these changes are no more than a minor face-lift. I do wish to emphasise that this book remains unchanged in substance and argument from its 1965 version. It has inevitably dated, and is not the book which I should now write. One shortcoming is technical. Now that new documents have stimulated further study of the Athenian cavalry (Braun 1970, Kroll 1977), it has become clear to me that service in the cavalry, nominally 1200 strong, can and should be used as an objective index of wealth closely comparable, in the level of wealth it presupposes, to membership of the trierarchic panel of 1200 under Periandros' law of 357 or to being named in the diadikasia-documents (See APF pp. xxvi-xxvii). Again, I should now alter some of the nuances in Chapter IV, 'The sources of wealth', so as to replace references to 'industrial' slave-owning by references to 'craftsman' or 'non-agricultural' slave-owning, and to emphasise more explicitly that non-agricultural sources of wealth should be seen only as supplements within a fundamentally agrarian society. A third shortcoming (if it is that) is more basic. For better or worse, the thesis did not make heavy weather of accommodating its approach within this or that theory of social description. Indeed, its approach is best seen as pre-theoretical, for my choice of interpretative themes to pursue - whether in terms of the values attached to behaviour denoted by significant words such as charis, philotimia, or dapane, or in terms of modern-language concepts such as cult-power and property-power - was the product of instinct rather than of real deliberation. I am aware too that the thesis did not start from what I would now see as the fundamental vectors of Athenian society (the needs for food, shelter, security, and conflict resolution), but concerned itself only with certain aspects of the behaviour of the upper economic class. In that sense the thesis cannot be seen as a proper structural analysis of Athenian society. All the same, it still seems to me, fifteen years later, that in its limited and over-empiricist way it does offer a coherent framework for understanding the interactions of a salient part of Athenian society. If criticism and argument can start from there, I am well content.

I wish to repeat my sense of obligation to all the persons and institutions mentioned in the Preface to APF. To them I add other and newer obligations : to Dr D.M. Lewis for further encouragement ; to Professor W.R. Connor for godfathering the inclusion of this thesis in the present series ; and to our Departmental secretary, Mrs Pat Sweetingham, for her professional care and personal helpfulness in the presentation of this typescript version.

J.K.D.

Liverpool, August 1980

ABBREVIATIONS

The only works listed here are those referred to in the text in an
abbreviated form : the list which follows should not be taken to comprise a
full bibliography. The titles of periodicals are abbreviated according to the
system of l'Annee philologique, save that a few have been expanded for clarity.
References to the editio minor of Inscriptiones Graecae are given in the form
'i²' for Volume I and 'ii²' for Volumes II–III.

Agora XVII   BRADEEN,D.W. The Athenian Agora, XVII : Inscriptions. The
              funerary monuments (Princeton, 1974)

Andrewes 1961 ANDREWES, A. 'Philochoros on phratries'. In JHS 81 (1961),
              1–15.

Andrewes 1962 ANDREWES, A. 'The Mytilene debate.' In Phoenix 16 (1972),
              64–85.

Andrewes 1978 ANDREWES, A. 'The opposition to Perikles.' In JHS 98
              (1978), 1–8.

APF   DAVIES, J.K. Athenian Propertied Families, 600–300 B.C.
              (Oxford, 1971)

Barron 1964   BARRON, J.P. 'Religious propaganda of the Delian league'.
              In JHS 84 (1964), 35 ff.

Bailey 1940   BAILEY, B.L. 'The export of Attic black-figure ware'. In
              JHS 60 (1940), 60–70.

Beauchet 1897 BEAUCHET, L. L'histoire du droit privé de la république
              athénienne (Paris, 1897)

Beazley 1946 BEAZLEY, J.D. Potter and painter in ancient Athens (PBA
              30)(London, 1946)

Beloch 1885   BELOCH, K.J. 'Das Volkvermögen von Attika'. In Hermes

20 (1885), 237–261.

Billeter 1898	BILLETER, G. _Geschichte des Zinsfusses_ (Leipzig, 1898)
Biscardi 1956	BISCARDI, A. 'Sul regime della comproprieta in diritto attico'. In _Studi in onore di Ugo Enrico Paoli_ (Firenze, 1956), 105–143.
Blass	BLASS, F. _Die attische Beredsamkeit_, I – III,2. 2nd ed. (Leipzig, 1887–1898)
Böckh 1886	BÖCKH, A. _Die Staatshaushaltung der Athener_, I – II. 3rd ed. (Berlin, 1886)
Bowra 1964	BOWRA, C.M. _Pindar_ (Oxford, 1964)
Braun 1970	BRAUN, K. 'Der Dipylon–Brunnen B$_1$: Die Funde'. In _AM_ 85 (1970), 129–269 at 197 ff.
Clerc 1893	CLERC, M. _Les métèques athéniens_ (Paris, 1893)
Connor 1971	CONNOR, W.R. _The new politicians of fifth–century Athens_ (Princeton, 1971)
Cook 1959	COOK, R.M. 'Die Bedeutung der bemalten Keramik für den griechischen Handel'. In _JDAI_ 74 (1959), 114–123.
DAA	RAUBITSCHEK, A.E. _Dedications from the Athenian akropolis_ (Cambridge, Mass. , 1949)
Daux 1963	DAUX, G. 'La grande démarchie : un nouveau calendrier sacrificiel d'Attique (Erchia)'. In _BCH_ 87 (1963), 603–634.
Davies 1967	DAVIES, J.K. 'Demosthenes on liturgies : a note'. In _JHS_ 87 (1967), 33–40.
Davies 1975	DAVIES, J.K. Review of Connor 1971 in _Gnomon_ 47 (1975), 374 ff.
Davies 1977-78	DAVIES, J.K. 'Athenian citizenship : the descent–group and the alternatives'. In _CJ_ 73 (1977–78), 105–121.
De Ste Croix 1953	DE STE CROIX, G.E.M. 'Demosthenes' TIMHMA and the Athenian eisphora in the fourth century B.C.'. In _Class. et Med._

14 (1953), 30-70.

De Ste Croix 1966   DE STE CROIX, G.E.M. 'The estate of Phaenippus (Ps.-Dem. xlii)'. In <u>Ancient society and institutions</u> (<u>Festschrift Ehrenberg</u>) (Oxford, 1966), 109-114.

Dow 1960   DOW, S. 'The Athenian calendar of sacrifices : the chronology of Nikomakhos' second term'. In <u>Historia</u> 9 (1960), 270-293.

Dow 1965   DOW, S. 'The greater demarkhia of Erchia'. In <u>BCH</u> 89 (1965), 180-213.

Dow 1968   DOW, S. 'Six Athenian sacrificial calendars'. In <u>BCH</u> 92 (1968), 170-186.

Eliot 1962   ELIOT, C.W.J. <u>The coastal demes of Attika</u> (Toronto, 1962)

Ferguson 1911   FERGUSON, W.S. <u>Hellenistic Athens</u> (London, 1911)

Fine 1951   FINE, J.V.A. <u>Horoi : studies in mortgage, real security, and land tenure in ancient Athens</u> (<u>Hesperia</u>, Suppl. IX) (Athens, 1951)

Finley 1952   FINLEY, M.I. <u>Studies in land and credit in ancient Athens, 500-200 B.C.</u> (New Brunswick, N.J., [1952])

Finley 1962   FINLEY, M.I. 'The Athenian demagogues'. In <u>Past and Present</u> 21 (1962), 3-24, reprinted in <u>Studies in ancient society</u> (ed. M.I. Finley) (London, 1974), 1-25.

Fornara 1971   FORNARA, C.W. <u>The Athenian board of generals from 501 to 404</u> (<u>Historia</u>, Einzelschrift 16) (Wiesbaden, 1971)

Geissler 1925   GEISSLER, P. <u>Chronologie der altattischen Komödie</u> (<u>Philol. Unt.</u> XXX) (Berlin, 1925)

Gerhardt 1933   GERHARDT, P. <u>Die attische Metoikie im viertem Jhdt.</u> (diss. phil. Königsberg Pr., 1933)

Gernet 1955   GERNET, L. <u>Droit et société dans la Grèce ancienne</u> (Paris, 1955)

Gernet 1968   GERNET, L. Anthropologie de la Grèce antique (Paris, 1968)

Glotz 1926   GLOTZ, G. Ancient Greece at work (London and New York, 1926)

GLP   PAGE, D.L. Greek literary papyri, I (London, 1942)

Gomme 1933   GOMME, A.W. The population of Athens in the fifth and fourth centuries B.C. (Oxford, 1933, repr. New York,1967)

Harrison 1968   HARRISON, A.R.W. The law of Athens, I : the family and property (Oxford, 1968)

Hauvette-Besnault 1885   HAUVETTE-BESNAULT, A. Les stratèges athéniens (Paris, 1885)

Hemelrijk 1925   HEMELRIJK, J. Πενία en Πλοῦτος (Diss. Utrecht, 1925)

Hignett 1952   HIGNETT, C. A history of the Athenian constitution (Oxford, 1952)

Jacoby 1956   JACOBY, F. Abhandlungen zur griechischen Geschichtschreibung, ed. H. Bloch (Leiden, 1956)

Jeffery 1948   JEFFERY, L.H. 'The boustrophedon sacral inscriptions from the Athenian Agora'. In Hesperia 17 (1948), 86 ff.

Jones 1957   JONES, A.H.M. Athenian democracy (Oxford, 1957)

Kahrstedt 1934   KAHRSTEDT, U. Staatsgebiet und Staatsangehörige in Athen, I (Stuttgart-Berlin, 1934)

Kalinka 1913   KALINKA, E. Die pseudo-Xenophontische Ἀθηναίων Πολιτεία (Leipzig-Berlin, 1913)

Kennedy 1963   KENNEDY, G.A. The art of persuasion in Greece (London, 1963)

Kraay and Emeleus 1962   KRAAY, C.M., and EMELEUS, V.M. The composition of Greek silver coins (Oxford, 1962)

Kraay 1964   KRAAY, C.M. 'Hoards, small change, and the origin of coinage'. In JHS 84 (1964), 76-91.

Kroll 1977   KROLL, J.H. 'An archive of the Athenian cavalry'. In Hesperia 46 (1977), 83-140.

Lewis 1954   LEWIS, D.M. 'Notes on Attic inscriptions, I'. In BSA 49

(1954), 17-50.

Lewis 1955   LEWIS, D.M. 'Notes on Attic inscriptions, II'. In BSA
50 (1955), 1-36.

Lewis 1959   LEWIS, D.M. 'Attic manumissions'. In Hesperia 28 (1959),
208-238.

Lewis 1961   LEWIS, D.M. 'Double representation in the strategia'. In
JHS 81 (1961), 118-123.

Lewis 1963   LEWIS, D.M. 'Cleisthenes and Attica'. In Historia 12
(1963), 22-40.

Lewis 1968   LEWIS, D.M. 'Dedications of phialai at Athens'. In
Hesperia 37 (1968), 368-380.

Lewis·1973   LEWIS, D.M. 'The Athenian Rationes Centesimarum'. In
Problèmes de la terre en Grèce ancienne, ed. M.I. Finley
(Paris-The Hague, 1973), 187-212.

Lipsius 1905-15 (MEIER, M.H.E., SCHÖMANN, G.F., and) LIPSIUS, J.H. Das
attische Recht und Rechtsverfahren (Leipzig, 1905-1915)

Meiggs 1964   MEIGGS, R. 'A note on the population of Attica'. In CR
78/14 (1964), 2-3.

Meritt 1962   MERITT, B.D. Greek historical studies (Cincinnati, 1962),
reprinted in Lectures in memory of Louise Taft Semple, first
series : 1961-1965, ed. D.W. Bradeen (Cincinnati, 1967),
95-132.

ML   MEIGGS, R., and LEWIS, D.M. A selection of Greek historical
inscriptions to the end of the fifth century B.C. (Oxford,
1969)

Möbius 1968   MÖBIUS, H. Die Ornamente der griechischen Grabstelen, 2nd
ed. (München, 1968)

PA   KIRCHNER, J. Prosopographia attica, I-II (Berlin, 1901-1903)

Pritchett 1946 PRITCHETT, W.K. 'Greek inscriptions'. In Hesperia 15

(1946), 138–165.

Pritchett 1956   PRITCHETT, W.K. 'The Attic Stelai, Part II'. In <u>Hesperia</u>
25 (1956), 178–317.

Schäfer   SCHÄFER, A. <u>Demosthenes und sein Zeit</u>, I–III, 2nd ed.
(Leipzig, 1885–1887)

Schlaifer 1940   SCHLAIFER, R. 'Notes on Athenian public cults'. In <u>HSCP</u>
51 (1940), 233–260.

Sokolowski 1962   SOKOLOWSKI, F. <u>Lois sacrées des cités grecques : supplément</u>
(Paris, 1962)

Sundwall 1906   SUNDWALL, J. <u>Epigraphische Beiträge zur sozial-politischen</u>
<u>Geschichte Athens</u> (<u>Klio</u>, Beiheft IV) (Leipzig, 1906)

Thompson 1968   THOMPSON, W.E. 'An interpretation of the "Demotionid"
decrees'. In <u>Symb. Osl.</u> 42 (1968), 51–68.

Thompson–   THOMPSON, M., MØRKHOLM, O., and KRAAY, C.M. <u>An inventory</u>
Mørkholm–Kraay   <u>of Greek coin hoards</u> (New York, 1973)
1973

Thomsen 1964   THOMSEN, R. <u>Eisphora</u> (Copenhagen, 1964)

Wade–Gery 1958   WADE–GERY, H.T. <u>Essays in Greek history</u> (Oxford, 1958)

Westermann 1955   WESTERMANN, W.L. <u>The slave systems of Greek and Roman</u>
<u>antiquity</u> (Philadelphia, 1955)

Whitehead 1977   WHITEHEAD, D. <u>The ideology of the Athenian metic</u> (<u>PCPhS</u>,
Suppl. 4) (Cambridge, 1977)

Wilamowitz 1893   WILAMOWITZ MOELLENDORF, U. von. <u>Aristoteles und Athen</u>, I–
II (Berlin, 1893)

Wyse 1904   WYSE, W. <u>The speeches of Isaeus</u> (Cambridge, 1904)

Chapter I

INTRODUCTION

This purports to be a social and economic study of the families
and individuals who formed the Athenian upper class. It has been the
product of two active influences in particular. The first was an
attitude of deep scepticism towards the claim, found, in one form or
another, in many ancient and some modern sources, to the effect that
under the advanced democracy the Athenian state was controlled from
below, by members of the artisan class. In face of, e.g. the Old
Oligarch's admission ([Xen.] Ath.Pol. i 3) that the major executive
offices were not filled by members of this class, to accept the claim
at its face value was to take an illegitimate short cut in analysing
the power structure of democratic Athens. Yet it was impossible to
assess the claim unless some way could be found of making a realistic
estimate of the actual economic and social position of those persons
who are known to have been active in public affairs, whether in office
or not.

The second influence, which pointed the same way, was a conscious-
ness that certain patterns of explanation, developed in the analysis of
political phenomena of other societies, might be profitably used - albeit
tentatively and provisionally - as analytical tools in the study of
Athenian history and society. I had three such analyses particularly in
mind: the first was Sir Lewis Namier's study 'The Structure of Politics
at the accession of George III' (London, 1929;[2] London, 1957), with its
emphasis on the unimportance of party labels and on politics as consisting mainly in the day-to-day filling of offices through patronage in
terms of nepotism, family influence, and amicitia. Secondly, Sir Ronald

2

Syme's The Roman Revolution (Oxford, 1939) had offered a description
of a political mi lieu where power was an end in itself rather than a
means to secure certain other ends of benefit to society as a whole or
to particular groups of it, and where the net effect of the Revolution
was the replacement of one ruling elite by another in 'a violent transfer
of power and property'. The third was the underlying idea of C. Wright
Mills' The Power Elite (New York, 1956), that, quite apart from formal
political structures there might exist a hierarchy of socio-economic
power, closely dependent on ownership and wealth, income and property.

I make no apology for seeking to apply these analyses to Athenian
society. Our evidence for Athens is such that it may at times be more
profitable to use it negatively, as a control on the applicability of
patterns developed elsewhere, than to use it positively as the basis
for an autarkic construct. Yet, at the outset, there was a factual
vacuum. One could not assess the prevalence of nepotism unless one
knew who was related to whom. One could not speak meaningfully about
discontinuities in the ruling elite or the political class unless one
could study its composition through many generations. One could not
begin to assess the importance of property-power unless one knew who
had property, and how much.

In consequence the largest part of this thesis, the Register [now APF],
consists simply in an attempt to supply a basis of factual knowledge,
in the light of which these, and other similar tentative analyses,
could be tested.

ii

It is not, naturally, the first such attempt. In 1906 J. Sundwall
published his Epigraphische Beiträge zur sozial-politischen Geschichte

Athens[1], with the declared purpose 'das sozial Niveau einiger
wesentlicher Verwaltungsbehörden sowie der munizipalen und allgemeinen
politischen Lebens zu betrachten' (p. V). To this end he assembled the
names of Athenians known to have held certain public positions in the
period 360-322 B.C., and tried to identify those who were 'reich' or
'wohlhabende'. As the first, and so far the only, systematic attempt
to apply an economic classification to even a cross-section of the
16,000-odd Athenians listed in Kirchner's Prosopographia Attica,
Sundwall's monograph has deserved well of later scholars.

However, it unfortunately suffered from certain deficiencies of
method. It is pertinent to specify them here, so that the desirable
characteristics of future work in this direction can be the more
narrowly re-defined.

(1) In the first place, the only persons discussed, with a few
exceptions, were those who were active within the years 360-322 B.C.
Sundwall had, indeed, some reason thus to confine his treatment,
since speeches and public documents survive in greater profusion from
those years than from any other comparable period of classical Athens.
On the other hand, evidence drawn from a period of little more than the
conventional generation cannot possibly provide the depth of focus
required to show change, either in the economic status of individuals
and families or in the recruiting field for particular offices. For
the social historian whose interest lies in this direction, it would
have been desirable to draw evidence from a period of at least a century,
and preferably more.

---

(1) Klio, Beiheft 4 (Leipzig, 1906).

4

(2)   Secondly, the two economic categories used by Sundwall, 'reich'
and 'wohlhabende' or 'Besitzende', derive from Beloch (1885, 257ff.).
The former group was equated by Sundwall (p. 2) with the 1200 persons
whom Beloch estimated to have owned property worth one _talent_ or more
and to have been equivalent to the Solonic pentakosiomedimnoi: the
latter group was equated (pp. 18 and 34) with the 9000 persons regarded
by Beloch (1885, 240) as being of the hoplite census. It is open to
question how far these categories or the labels given to them accurately
reflect the main actual contemporary social and economic divisions in
Athens. It is true, as Böckh noted (1886, 590) that the Solonic
classifications still existed and continued to be used for certain
purposes in the fourth-century, but there is very little evidence that
fourth-century Athenians thought or legislated primarily in such terms.[2]
Aristotle thought it worthy of remark that in the 320's the tamiai of
Athene were still selected from among the pentakosiomedimnoi, and implies
moreover that a person so selected could be 'very poor' (πάνυ πένης)
(Ath.Pol. xlvii 1). The orators, who may certainly be regarded as
providing the best evidence for contemporary political terminology,
almost invariably speak in terms of 'rich' (πλούσιοι) and 'poor' (πένητες),
'well-provided' (εὔποροι) and 'beggars' (πτωχοί), but it cannot be
assumed without detailed analysis that those whom the orators called
'rich' or 'well-provided' are identical with those whom Sundwall called
'reich'.

(3)   In an investigation of the kind undertaken by Sundwall it needs to
be decided at the outset what does and what does not constitute good

---

(2)   Such references as survive are collected by de Ste Croix   1953, 42.

evidence that a particular given Athenian was in a particular economic class.
Sundwall did not explicitly do this, and indeed not infrequently stretched
the available evidence in order to allocate a person to a particular
economic category. I give two examples.

(a) Grave-monuments are frequently adduced as evidence that the deceased or
his family was of good financial standing. In other circumstances such
evidence might be useful and acceptable, though attested costs for grave-
monuments vary enormously (see APF p.xix n.3) and cannot be reliably corre-
lated with a monument of given known style and complexity. However, it so
happens that the latter half of Sundwall's chosen period, the years 340-317,
saw such an increase in the number and elaborateness of style of grave-
monuments as to call forth Demetrios' sumptuary legislation of 317 (Ferguson
1911,42; Möbius 1968, 39 and 44 n.50). Consequently it is during just this
period that the evidential value of grave-monuments is least reliable.

(b) In assessing the financial position of a man active during the period
360-322, Sundwall tended to employ evidence pertaining to ancestors or descendants. For example Lysimachos (II) of Myrrhinous, councillor after 350
(Agora XV 32, line 28), is counted as 'wohlhabend' (p.8) on the ground that an
ancestor, Lysimachos (I) (PA 9523), was archon in 436/5: and Eukleides of
Aithalidai, councillor in (?) 370/69 (Agora XV 13, line 108), is surmised to
have been 'wohlhabend' (p.4) on the ground that a descendant was an ephebe
in 123/2. The dangers of inferences from such evidence are manifest. There
is good reason for thinking that homonymity within a deme is not necessarily
a good ground for presupposing relationship,[3] while in the face of apparent

---

(3) Cf. the two men named Nikostratos of Halai (see APF 3126), the confusion
   of Δημμ -homonyms in Paiania (see APF 3597, §1), and the several men from
   Euonymon named Stephanos (see APF 12888 and Pritchett 1946, 164).

counter-examples the continuity of a family, or the stability of its economic circumstances, cannot be assumed without either positive individual evidence, or statistically, the kind of demographic analysis which so far has never been applied to Athens.

iii

The compilation of the Register is meant, at least in intention, to meet these dangers and shortcomings. Its basis is provided by members of a specified class, definable economically with some attempt at quantitative precision in terms of a reliable and practicable criterion. This class is the propertied class, the one or two per cent of Athenian citizens whose wealth placed them at the top of the Athenian economic structure. I chose to concentrate attention on this class for three reasons. First, for it as for no other class a reliable criterion was available which was likely to offer an effective sorting-out mechanism. Secondly, what was known about this class was likely to be better in quality and quantity than that known about other groups: this has proved to be true. Thirdly, the study of this class was more likely than that of any other to be politically relevant: if, for example, there were found to be offices, between the holders of which and this class there was no significant overlap, this would be an important and valuable negative result. Conversely, the more overlaps there were between this class and known generals, or known proxenoi, or known politicians, the more justifiable would it become to speak of the Athenian propertied class as being also the governing class.

By this means the second and third criticisms levelled above against Sundwall's monograph can be effectively met. The first criticism,

that of a too limited time-span, has been met in two ways. First,
evidence has been taken from a period of about 300 years. The
starting point has been taken as the time (ca. 600 B.C.) when the
importance of, and interest in, a man's personal property had
increased to the point where not only do statements about the
economic position of individual persons begin to be recorded, but
also the institutions of the state begin to be ordered in terms of
personal property rather than of inherited aristocratic rank. The
terminal point (about 300 B.C.) is roughly that at which the criteria
of selection for the Register fail, and at which the disappearance of
the Athenian navy as a wielder of effective power in the Aegean had
imposed upon Athens new and different forms of political expression.
These limits are necessarily arbitrary, and it need hardly be pointed
out that the evidence about persons is not spread evenly throughout
the period, so that there is a serious risk of distortion in the picture
of the class. This is inevitable, but not, I hope, lethal.

The second way of meeting the first criticism consists in considering the men who qualify for the Register not simply as individuals but
as members of a family, with relatives, forebears and descendants, whose
economic and social position may have changed in the course of time.
Hence the families of these men have been traced as far as the evidence
allows, and the evidence for the property of the various relatives
described in as much detail as possible. This will provide some kind
of factual basis for assessing the stability and continuity of the
families concerned and the importance or otherwise of inter-family
relationships.

The information contained in the Register is therefore limited, in

two respects. First, the Register has no pretensions to being a
complete prosopography, and lists only the members of the Athenian
propertied class together with their certain or probable relatives.
Secondly, the descriptions of each family concentrate on two foci
of attention:

(i) the evidence for the financial standing of the family, and for
changes in this standing;

(ii) the evidence for the genealogy of the family. This includes
evidence for details of relationships and for the dates of births,
marriages, and deaths. Known descendants and ancestors have usually
been included for the sake of a complete picture, even when their
periods of activity lie outside the years 600-300: but for some few
families, e.g. those of Lykourgos of Boutadai and Diodoros of Halai,
many of the members of which were active in the Hellenistic period, it
was impossible to do so without occupying disproportionate space.

In the case of families or persons about whom comparatively little
is known, I have attempted to give the complete corpus of evidence
pertaining to them. However, for men or families about whom a good
deal is known (e.g. many politicians and generals), I have not attempted
to describe public careers except insofar as they throw light on one
or other of the two foci of interest. The decision in border-line
cases has not been easy to make, and anomalies no doubt remain, for
which apology is offered here: but not to make such decisions would
have destroyed the whole purpose of the undertaking.

Chapter II

THE LITURGICAL CENSUS

i

By far the best available means of obtaining a precise picture of
the composition of the Athenian propertied class is to compile a list of
those known to have performed at least one State liturgy. Economically,
the choice of this criterion needs little defence. Its reliability is
guaranteed, in the first place, by the very financial outlay involved,
which ranged from 300 dr. for a Panathenaic chorus[1] to a talent for a
sole trierarchy.[2] Even the cheapest liturgy cost nearly as much as a
contemporary skilled workman was paid in a year (APF p.xxii n.6), while
the most expensive liturgies involved spending three times as much as the
fourth-century hoplite census if Jones (1957, 79f. and 142 n.50) was
right in taking 2000 dr. to be the amount of property required to reach
hoplite status. Hence the performance of such duties was beyond the means
of all but a very small proportion of the Athenian citizen body.

Furthermore, the procedures of diadikasia and antidosis, both well
attested throughout the century from the 420's to the 320's if not before,[3]

---

(1) Lys. xxi 2 (in 409/8). The eutaxia-liturgy was even cheaper (50 dr)
but is only attested once (ii^2 417) and was probably short-lived.

(2) Dem. xxi 155. For the cost of the various liturgies see APF pp.xxi-xxii.

(3) For the evidence see APF xxii nn.7-8.

helped to ensure the reliability of this criterion by providing mechanisms
whereby changes in the economic circumstances of individuals could be
translated into a change in the composition of the liturgical class.
Though sharp practices certainly occurred (see APF p.xxii n.9), and
though the antidosis-procedure was cumbrous and depended on the
initiative and personal knowledge of the aggrieved party, the mechanisms
seem to have worked well enough to ensure that at any one time there was
no major discrepancy between the liturgical class and the class of the
richest Athenians. If some marginal cases are allowed for, the inference
from a man's performance of a liturgy to the pre-eminence of his economic
position at the time is secure enough for the risk of serious error to be
negligible.

Almost as valuable, though more adventurous, is the argument from
terminology. Hemelrijk argued persuasively (1925, 1-52) that the words
πλούσιοι ('rich') and πένητες ('poor') describe, not so much two polar-
ized groups at opposite ends of the social scale, as two overlapping groups
which do not by themselves cover the whole economic range. The 'poor'
(πένητες) are not the destitute, who are 'beggars' (πτωχοί) or 'needy'
(δεόμενοι or ἐνδεεῖς), but those who have to work for their living; the
better-off in this class are called sometimes 'rich', sometimes 'poor',
while the 'rich' (πλούσιοι or εὔποροι) are the rentier class or the leisure
class, and the class which bears the financial burdens of the state.[4]
This is, I think, true, but one may tentatively go a little further.
Aristotle let slip, as his definition of the second highest class in the

---

(4) Hemelrijk 1925, 52-4; German summary, 140-2.

state, the revealing phrase "The seventh (constituent part of a state)
is that section which serves the state with its properties: we call
it 'rich' (εὐπόρουϲ)" (Pol. 1291ᵃ 33-4). If due allowance is made for
rhetorical cliches, forensic tricks (see APF xxi nn.2-3) and the natural
elasticity of the word 'rich', Aristotle's definition on the whole holds
true: most of the individuals called 'rich' (πλούϲιοϲ or εὐποροϲ) are
in the liturgical class, with hardly anybody demonstrably outside it,[5]
and there is a widespread tendency in Athenian sources to speak of 'the
wealthy'(οἱ πλούϲιοι or οἱ εὐποροι) or of 'those who possess property'
(οἱ τὰ κτήματ' ἐχοντεϲ) as a group virtually identical in composition to
'the trierarchs' or to 'those who perform liturgies',

The point is best made by quotation. The Old Oligarch is explicit:
'In the matter of the training and staging of performers for dramatic and
choral performances, the training and staging of athletic team contests,
and the commissioning and command of warships, (the common people) realise
that it is the rich who provide the choregia, and the people who are
provided for; that is the rich who perform gymnasiarchies and trierarchies,
while the people have them performed for them' ([Xen.] Ath.Pol. i 13).
A generation later a client of Lysias, trying to arouse prejudice against
the nouveaux riches of the Korinthian War, who included his opponent
Epikrates, complained how 'they were poor once, and have got rich in the
war at your expense, while you yourselves have become poor because of them.
It is not the task of honest politicians to appropriate your goods while you
suffer disaster, but rather to give you what is their own. Yet we have got
to the point where men who formerly in peacetime could not even maintain
themselves are now paying you special tax-levies, performing choregiai, and
living in large houses ' (Lys. xxvii 9-10).

---

(5) See APF p.xxi n.4 for a possible exception.

This extraordinary maladroit passage, which, by complaining of the
social rise of the nouveaux riches, gives away the essential point
that they made no bones about performing the civic duties appropriate
to their new status,[6] reveals by this very admission how closely the
notion of being wealthy was bound up with, and identified with, the payment of eisphora and the performance of liturgies. Later, again, about
360 the terminology of Isaios shows the same thing, by describing two
brothers as 'not among those who perform liturgies.... but among those
who possess modest property' (Isaios xi 48: see APF 2921, XII), while a
few years later Isokrates pinpointed, as the evil result of the Social
War, 'the mass of instructions and liturgies and the evils attendant
upon the special tax-levy panels and suits about exchanges of property.
They cause such anguish that property-owners live more wretchedly than
men in continuous poverty' (Isok.viii Peace 128): clearly, for Isokrates,
the 'property-owners' are identical with the liturgical class. Demosthenes'
terminology points the same way. In 348 friends of Meidias had warned him
against taking his quarrel with Meidias to court, saying 'Do you not see
that he is wealthy and will quote his trierarchies and liturgies (in court)?'
(Dem. xxi 151). The virtual synonymity recurs later in the speech, where
some of those who were going to beg Meidias off are described as 'rich
and trierarchs' (Dem.xxi 208): it is fitting that the three men whom
Demosthenes names, Philippides, Mnesarchides, and Diotimos, are all
independently attested as trierarchs. Most illuminating of all is his
description of his own naval reform of 340. The result of the Periandric
regime had been that 'the rich were coming off tax-free after trivial

---

(6) Cf. Lys. xix 28-29 for a precisely parallel case, where Lysias is
    writing for the other side.

contributions, while those citizens who possessed modest or little property where destroying what they had' (Dem.xviii 102), for 'the performance of liturgies lay with the poor' (7). By his own reform, in contrast, 'I compelled one group, the rich, to act justly, and I stopped the poor from being unjustly treated' (Dem.xviii 102).

It is an extraordinary fact that, in terms of this description, all but the richest 300 of the 1200 richest men in the State are 'poor' or 'without resources' (ἄπορει : Dem.xviii 104). Admittedly, this is a persuasive definition, just as the parrot-cry ascribed to Meidias, 'we are the men who perform liturgies, we are the men who pay special tax-levies in advance for you, we are the rich men' (Dem.xxi 153), is intended as a caricature. Yet Demosthenes had said much the same thing in 355(8) at a time when he was not perceptibly acting on behalf of the 'poor', and the other passages quoted above show both that the distortions involved are not violent, and that Aristotle's definition had a solid foundation in ordinary usage. In some sense, then, the members of the liturgical class could be regarded as forming a class by themselves, roughly co-terminous with 'the rich' (πλούσιοι or εὔποροι), rather than as a privileged sub-section of a larger class the members of which had an equal right to the title 'rich'. The many who were in the rentier or leisure class, but not rich enough to be 'men who perform liturgies', are not, on the whole, called 'rich': like Stratokles, they owned 'enough.... for it to be adequate, but not enough to perform liturgies' (Isaios xi 40). In contrast, the selection of the 'men who

---

(7) Dem.xviii 108. Cf. the statement put into the mouth of Leptines in 355: 'the liturgies are now coming on to the poor men' (Dem. xx 18).

(8) Dem.xx 18, quoted in note 7 above.

14

perform liturgies' to embody the Athenian propertied class is the
selection, not of an amorphous, arbitrarily defined group of men at the
top of the economic scale, but that of a group which, with its special
burdens, responsibilities, and privileges, formed a recognized social
class. This is not to say that it was a caste, since its composition was
subject to continual change, still less that it was a politically
cohesive group, [9] but only that in studying it as a unity we shall
not be doing gross violence to the sociological and economic facts as they
were observed and described by the Athenians themselves.

---

(9) The indications that it was (Hell.Ox. vi 3 Bart. etc.) are discussed
in Chapter VI.

Chapter III

THE LITURGICAL CLASS

The determination of the size of the liturgical class, and the
determination of the minimum level of wealth required for adscription
into it, are two distinct but closely inter-related problems, to both of
which some solution must be offered here if the picture of the liturgical
class is not to be merely qualitative. It is necessary to discuss both
at some length. This is partly because discussion of the second problem
has been sensibly impeded in the past by the misinterpretation of one of
the principal relevant texts, and partly because the most recent discussion
of the first problem, that by A.H.M. Jones (1957, 85f), has presented as
normal a figure which is, I think, a major anomaly and must be seen as such
and discounted.

i

It is convenient to take first the question of the size of the class.
Here a sharp distinction must be made between military liturgies (i.e. the
trierarchy and the proeisphora) and agonistic liturgies, for we have firm
figures only for the number of men liable to military liturgies. The
relevant figures are as follows.

(i) The Athenian fleet at Artemision[1] and at Salamis [2] in
480 numbered 180 ships. Since we cannot assume that the 20 Athenian hulls
manned by Chalkidians in both battles[3] had Athenian trierarchs, 180 can
safely be taken as the number of Athenian trierarchs involved in that year.

---

(1) 127 (Hdt.viii 1,1) plus the 53 reinforcements (Hdt.viii 14,1).

(2) Hdt. viii, 44,1.

(3) Hdt. viii 1,2 and viii 46,2.

(ii) Plutarch's statement (Perikles xi 4), in a context of the 440's, that 60 ships were in commission for eight months of every year, and Thucydides' report (ii 24,2) of the Athenian decision in 431 to keep a reserve fleet of the 100 best ships in commission and in reserve every year, give some background figures of current practice, but clearly cannot be used even as minimum estimates of the size of the trierarch- ical class. [In any case the historicity and reliability of Plutarch's information is open to serious doubt (Andrewes 1978, 1ff).]

(iii) In the 420's '400 trierarohs are appointed each year' ([Xen.] Ath. Pol. iii 4). As Kalinka's excellent note ad loc. (Kalinka 1913, 280f.) makes clear, the difficulty in this explicit and invaluable statement is that Athens in 431 had rather over 300 ships in service, not 400,[4] so that the necessity for the higher figure is not apparent. The answer probably lies, not in supposing that allowance was made for subsequent diadikasiai and antidoseis (for these would not reduce the total number on the generals' list), but in supposing that the known fourth-century rule whereby a man could not be obliged - or was not allowed - to perform two liturgies simultaneously[5] also obtained in the fifth century. The figure of 400 would then allow the men (one hundred or so: see below) who were performing an agonistic liturgy in any one year to claim exemption, and, even if they all did so, it would still provide enough trierarchs

---

(4) Thuc. ii 13, 8; Ar.Ach.545; Xen.Anab. vii 1,27 (where however the deteriores have τετρακοσίων); Aisch. ii 175. And. iii 9 records 'over 400' but the context is the Peace of Nikias and the test has been doubted.

(5) Dem. xx 19 and xxi 155; [Dem.] 1 9.

for a full moibilization of the fleet. Hence, and since we know that, in contrast, the fourth-century exemption-rule of one (Dem.xx8) or two (Isaios vii 38) years between successive liturgies did not apply in the fifth century[6], the Old Oligarch's figure of 400 can safely be taken to represent the size of the trierarchical class in the 420's. (iv) From 378/7 until presumably 322 there existed by the side of the trierarchy a second military liturgy, known by 360 as the proeisphora (special advance tax-levy), to which 300 persons (including minors) were liable at any one time.

There is a margin of uncertainty in this statement, but it has been so much reduced by the analysis of Ste. Croix (1953, 30ff.), with which I entirely agree, of the problems of the fourth-century eisphora that only a very summary treatment is necessary here. It is beyond dispute (a) that those liable to the proeisphora were 300 in number in the period from ca. 350 onwards[7] and (b) that the proeisphora was a liturgy in the 320's ([Dem.] xlii 3-5 and 25). The only problem is whether these propositions can be taken to have been true right from the initiation

---

(6) Isaios vii 38 'οὐδὲ δύο ἔτη διαλιπὼν ἀλλὰ cυνεχῶc ' ('nor with a gap of two years but continuously'). Similarly, the speaker of Lysias xxi was trierarch for seven years continuously, from 411/0 til 405, but there are dangers in taking his career as typical (see APF D7).

(7) For προειcφέροντεc in the 340's cf. Dem. xxi 153 and xxxvii 37. The only reference to the number 300 in the same decade is Dem. ii 29, but it can hardly refer to anything else.

of the symmory-system in 378/7.[8] The basic evidence is twofold;
in describing the eisphora of September 362, Apollodoros implied that
the proeisphora was a liturgy ([Dem] 1 9),and two years earlier, in 364,
it was said of two men (father and son) that they had both paid all the
eisphorai "in the Three Hundred", and of a third (a younger son) that
he had been enrolled "into the Three Hundred" and was paying all the
eisphorai (Isaias vi 60). Ste Croix (1953, 58f.) is unquestionably
right to say: "The original intention of the inventors of the symmory
system must have been to provide a series of small, clearly defined
bodies of men, from each of which a wealthy proeispheron could recoup
himself for the advance he had made on their behalf", and hence that
"the proeisphora must have been the main object of the 378 reform".
Hence, and since the total number of eisphora-payers was certainly much
larger than 300, Isaios' Three Hundred must have occupied a special
position, and fulfilled a special function, within the general body of
eisphora-payers; and it is next to impossible to see what this function
can have been but that performed by the group later known as the

---

(8) Philochoros, FGH 328 F 41. (I note for completeness' sake the
    attempt by Thomsen (1964, 85ff and 114ff) to invoke Kleidemos FGH 323F 8
    as evidence against Philochoros' explicit statements. I shall hope to
    show elsewhere that the argument is quite misguided, and that
    Philochoros' evidence and the communis opinio should stand.

Residual problems remain[9], but are not serious enough to affect
the main point; the number of those liable to the second military
liturgy was consistently 300 from 378/7 till 322.

(v) Periandros' naval law of ca. 357, which extended the symmory
organisation from the eisphora to the navy, set up a panel of 1200 persons
liable to the trierarchy (Isok. xv 145: Dem.xiv 16).

(vi) Demosthenes' naval law of 340 transferred the trierarchical burden
to the 300 'richest men' (Hypereides F 134). By the 320's, probably
indeed by Demosthenes' law, the panel of the 300 men liable to the
trierarchy and the panel of the 300 men liable to the proeisphora
were effectively identical ([Dem.] xlii 3-5 and 25) and formed the two
aspects of a class, 300 in number, which financed and performed the
military liturgies.

This picture calls for three remarks. In the first place, it becomes
probably that throughout the fifth and fourth centuries the size of the
class which performed the military liturgies was always of the order of
200-400, except that during the period from 357 till 340 a much larger
class, 1200 in number, took over the trierarchy. Seen against the background of the previous 150 years, Periandros' reform, the reasons for
which are still dismally obscure, stands out as a major shifting of the
trierarchical burden on to the backs of men some of whom could without
gross implausibility be described as 'poor' (Dem.xviii 102-108). Like

---

(9) E.g. that of explaining why the symmory-system of proeisphora was by-
    passed in 362 (for a possible answer, see Appendix I), that of explain-
    ing what monies Adrotion's commission was collecting ca. 356, or that
    of explaining what had happened to the symmories for Demosthenes to be
    able to say in 349 " πρότερον εἰσεφέρετε κατὰ cυμμορίας " (Dem.ii 29).

the number 1200, such terminology finds no parallel, as a characterization of the trierarchical class, either before 357 or after 340. Only one inference can be drawn; far from creating a new, and unprecedentedly restricted class of men liable to the trierarchy, Demosthenes' law merely rectified a serious anomaly by restoring and systematizing the status quo. The "normal" size of the trierarchical class must be taken, not with Jones as 1200, but as being of the order of 300.

Secondly, since the varying figures for the "normal" size of this class are the result of rational legislative decisions, it is pertinent to enquire what the grounds for these decisions were. The obvious and necessary answer is that these figures were a function of the resources of the country, but it is not at once apparent whether the limit was set by the availability of ships, of men, or of money. The first possibility can be excluded, since, given the wood, there was nothing to prevent an unlimited number of ships being built. More important, the operative limit in terms of manpower seems to have been such that at no time except 480 did the number of ships in commission even approach the number of men in the trierarchical class at the time. This is shown by the known maximum figures of ships simultaneously at sea: 180 at Artemision and Salamis in 480;[10] 160 at the end of the Samian revolt in 440/39;[11] rather over 130 in summer 431; [12] rather over 218 in Spring

---

(10) See p. 15 above.

(11) 60 (Thuc. i 116, 1) plus 40 (Thuc. i 116, 2) plus 40 (Thuc. i 117, 2) plus 20 (Thuc. i 117, 2).

(12) 100 ships round Peloponnese (Thuc. ii 23, 2 etc.) plus 30 round Lokris and Euboia (Thuc. ii 26, 1) plus an unknown number concerned in the operations on Aigina (Thuc. ii 27).

413;[13]   110 at Arginousai in 406 (Xen. Hell. i 6, 24); over 140 at Aigospotamoi in 405;[14]   120 at Embata in 356 (Diod. xvi 21,1); and 170 in summer 322 (Diod.xviii 15,8). Some of these figures certainly, and others probably, represent the maximum number of ships which could be manned at the time. The shortfall between them and the contemporary size of the triararchical class is such that, had the size of the class been determined merely or primarily with reference to the number

---

(13) The 100 ships of the first fleet to Sicily (Thuc. vi 31, 3 etc.) plus
     10 under Eurymedon (Thuc. vii 16, 2) plus 30 under Charikles (Thuc.
     vii 20, 1) plus 60 under Demosthenes (Thuc. vii 20, 2) plus 30 under
     Charikles (Thuc. vii 20, 1) plus 60 under Demosthenes (Thuc. vii 20, 2)
     plus 18 under Konon (Thuc. vii 31, 4) plus an unknown but probably
     small number at Pylos (Thuc. vi 105, 2 and vii 18, 3). The 20 ships
     sent round Peloponnese in December 414 (Thuc. vii 17, 2) mysteriously
     disappear in the subsequent narrative, and should probably not be
     added to the total. Either they returned to Athens before
     Demosthenes set out, or (much more likely: see Dover ad loc.) they
     became Konon's 18 at Naupaktos (Thuc. vii 31, 4). The six extra
     ships which made the fleet at Naupaktos under Diphilos up to 33 (Thuc.
     vii 34, 3) had presumably come with Diphilos when he as general for
     413/2 relieved Konon (thus Dover ad loc.).

(14) The total of 180 (Xen.Hell. ii 1, 20; Diod. xiii 105, 1) presumably
     included the survivors of the 40 allied ships at Arginousai (Xen.
     Hell. i 6, 25).

of ships which could be simultaneously manned, it could or should have
been very much smaller than it was.

Consequently, the evidence suggests that the size of the class was
at least partly, and perhaps primarily determined in terms of some other
factor than the availability of ships or manpower. I suggest that this
factor is financial: the "normal" size of the class was deliberately
set thus so as to correspond with the maximum number of men in Athens
who could afford the drain on their personal incomes involved in being
a trierarch. Some proof of this is forthcoming from the narrowness of
the margin. The coupling of two men together as syntrierarchs, a
practice which is first attested during the Dekeleian War, possibly at
Arginousai,[15] implies official recognition of the fact that at the
post-412 level of the national income the more moderately well-off
members of the class had ceased to be able to meet their obligations
singly. Fifty years later, when the size of the trierarchical class was
greatly increased by Periandros' reform and when the burden was being
spread evenly,[16] rather than proportionally, among the members of this
enlarged class, the result was, as it had to be, trierarchs 'by fives
and sixes' (cùv πέντε καì ἕξ)[17] or even 'by sixteens' (cùv ἑκκαιδεκα :
Dem. xviii 104): the poorer members could not meet the obligation save

---

(15) Lys. xxxii 24 and 26-27 (see APF 3885); ii²1951 passim.

(16) This is a reasonable inference from the close homogeneity of the
debts recorded in ii²1622, lines 580f.

(17) Hypereides F 134; ii²1622, lines 580f., particularly lines
611 f. (a group of seven) and 623f. (a group of eight).

in large groups. The "normal" size of the class left little to spare;
it was the maximum number of men who could reasonably be asked to be
executive trierarchs. The change from the 420's, when 400 men could
each meet the obligation singly, to the period after 340, when 300
men could meet the obligation, usually in pairs or threes, reflects
the decline in Athens' capital resources, but the principle of selection
for the two bodies remained, I think, the same.

A third remark remains to be made. The proeisphora was established
in 378/7, and functioned in terms of a 100-symmory tax system,[18] but
there is no perceptible reason, inherent in the system, why the persons
liable to the proeisphora should have been 300 in number rather than any
other multiple of 100 or even 100 itself. The reason for the choice of
the figure 300 lies, I suspect, in an analogous calculation; 300 was
the maximum number of persons[19] whose resources allowed them to fulfil
the role expected of them, viz., money-raising on a large scale in a
hurry. They, and only they, could raise eranos-loans, or mortgage
property, or had ready money available at home or in banks, on such a
scale that among them they could advance tothe State the 50 tal. or more

---

(18) Kleidemos, FGH 323 F8; Philochoros, FGH 328 F 41; Ste Croix 1953, 56f.
(19) Strictly speaking, 300 property-units, since 'incapables' (ἀδύνατοι)
such as Demosthenes during his minority were not excluded from the
roster.

which would be expected from an eisphora.[20] . In sum, it looks as if
the figures of 400, in part of the fifth century, or of 300, for much
of the fourth century, are not arbitrarily selected as the size of
the class that performed the military liturgies. They were, on the
contrary, in some sense natural and inescapable, the observed or
presumed approximate maximum size of the class that had the financial
resources to perform them satisfactorily. The one recorded attempt to
alter its size, that of Periandros, was a disastrous failure. Hence,
these figúres yield important information about property distribution
in Athens. In the 420's about 400 people, and not many more, could
afford a drain on their income of up to 1 tal. a year for the military
purposes of the State: in the fourth century about 300 people, and not
many more, could afford a drain on their income of up to 3000 dr. a year
for such purposes.

The agonistic liturgies present a slightly different picture. Lists
of trierarchs certainly existed and were continuously kept up to date
by the generals.[21] In contrast, no such lists were kept of those
liable to agonistic liturgies.[22] This point, demonstrable for the

---

(20)I follow Ste Croix 1953, 50, in his assumption that a levy of less
than 0.5% of the timema of the country would not have been worth
the trouble of collecting; nor would a smaller levy than 50 tal.
be much use for a military or naval expedition large enough to
warrant an eisphora in the first place.

(21) Ar.Knights 912f. with scholiast ad loc.; Dem. xxxix 8; Dem. xxxv 48;
Ath.Pol. lxi l; ii²1629, lines 204f; [Dem.] xlii 5; Suda H 39.

(22) For the one apparent, but not real, exception to this statement, viz.
the diadikasia-documents (ii²1928-1932), see Appendix I.

fourth century, can be safely extrapolated backwards into the fifth

century. Aischines, in describing the property which Timarchos

inherited, said that Timarchos' father had left him property 'from

which another man would even have performed liturgies' (Aisch. i 97):

such language entails that it lay within Timarchos' field of choice

whether to perform liturgies or not. Similarly, Demosthenes' comparison

of his own liturgical record with that of Meidias (Dem.xxi 154f.) had no

forensic point unless the two men could up to a point choose, even with

the trierarchy, whether to perform a particular liturgy or not. Again

the failure of choregoi to come forward for the context in comedy at the

Dionysia in 390/89 (Platonios ap. Meineke, Com.Frag. I 532) and the

similar failure of choregoi in Pandionis for the men's dithyrambic

contests in 349/8[23] are inexplicable unless the archon responsible for

the Dionysia, or the tribal authorities, were dependent upon men coming

forward or being nominated, had no list of reserves who could be called

upon, and could not exercise compulsion. There were, it is true, pen-

alties for the non-performance of liturgies (Dem.xxxix 8), but it is

important to note that these apparently applied only after a man had

been appointed to the liturgy by the appropriate authorities. So too

the language of Isaios v 36 implies that Dikaiogenes had tried to

escape nomination (see Wyse ad loc. and And. i 132), evidently with some

success. Perhaps the clearest evidence is provided by a four-line epigram

---

(23) Dem. xxi 13. This fact made nonsense of Demosthenes' own confident
     prediction in 355/4 that 'there will be many men to perform
     liturgies, providing that the city is in being: the supply of
     them will not fail' (Dem.xx 22).

from Vari, ii^{2}3101, set up in the second half of the fourth century
by a man of Anagyrous whose victory in comedy at the City Dionysia
prompted his father to emulate him and to gain a Dionysiac victory
himself (see APF A21).   Here the son's successful challenge to his
father's quiescence implies that it depended very largely on the
father himself to choose whether or not to put himself forward for a
liturgy. We misunderstand the workings of the agonistic liturgical
system if we approximate it to a super-tax, as an automatic recurrent
imposition on fortunes over a certain size. On the contrary, the
element of choice, and of appeal to, and reliance upon, the generosity
and philotimia of the individual, always formed a very far from
negligible part of the system. That the motivation behind such
generosity and philotimia was essentially practical - the hope of a
political or forensic return - is undeniable and, I believe, crucial
(see Chapter VI below), and the recalcitrant were always liable to
the sanction of an antidosis-challenge, but even Aristotle had to
admit that the abolition of agonistic liturgies would have to be
brought about in the teeth of men 'who actually wish to perform
liturgies' (Pol. 1309^a 17). The nexus of thought was encapsulated in
the dedication made by a fourth-century victor at the Panathenaia and
(with a boys' chorus) at the Thargelia: 'by setting such examples to his
own children he is stimulating them to reach out further towards
excellence' (ii^{2}3022: Τοιάδε τις δείξας παραδε[ί]γματα παιcίν
ἑαυτῶ | μᾶλλον ὀρέξεcθαι τῆc ἀρετῆc προτρέπει).
In such a context, compulsion and arete are mutually exclusive.

The consequence of this is that the agonistic liturgical class was
at once more amorphous and more open-ended than the trierarchical class.

It is no accident that the only figure we have for the size of the
agonistic liturgical class applies not to its absolute size but to
the number of such liturgies performed each year. This figure was
given by Demosthenes in 355/4 as rather over 60 liturgies a year
(Dem.xx 21). Böckh (1886, I 538) doubted it as being a serious
underestimate. [The exposition which followed here was set out in
detail in JHS 87 (1967) 33-40, and need not be repeated here. The
conclusion which emerges is that Böckh's doubts were justified, since]
the sum total of appointments to festival liturgies appears to have
been over 97 annually at the time of Dem. xx, rising to over 118 in
a Panathenaic year. Two observations can be made which support the
revised figure. First, if, as is likely, the figure can be extrapolated back to the time of the Old Oligarch, it accounts almost
exactly for the gap between the size of the fleet and the number of
trierarchs appointed annually, and such a close fit is unlikely to be
coincidental. Secondly, the revised figure, when taken with the
fourth-century exemption rules providing for one or two years between
successive liturgies (p. 6 above), requires that the agonistic liturgical
class must have been of the order of 200 or 300, and this is so close
to the 'normal' size of the trierarchical class as to suggest that it
is the same class under another aspect. Hence, in spite of the
differences in recruitment and definition, it looks as if there was
at any one time a virtual identity in size and composition between the
class of men who performed the agonistic or festival liturgies and the
class who performed the trierarchy; from both points of view it
comprised a group of about 300 men. This is 1% of the standard fifth-
century figure of 30,000 for the male citizen population of Athens,

and 1.4% of the figure of 21,000 attested for Athens in 316.

ii

The second defining characteristic of the liturgical class, the
level of wealth required for ascription into it, can be defined
fairly narrowly for the fourth century. The relevant evidence, in
approximate chronological order, is set out in APF pp. xxiii-xxiv, and
need not be repeated here. With the exception of Isaios v 35-36 (which
must be either a gross anomaly or, more likely, a gross misrepresentation
of the facts), it is consistent with the supposition that during the
fourth century men whose property was worth less than 3 tal. were free
from liturgical obligations, while men whose property was worth over
4 tal. were very unlikely to escape such obligations in the long run.
It is very probable that the corresponding figures for the fifth
century were rather higher, but there is no evidence to indicate by
how much.

This picture receives some confirmation from the statement made
by the speaker of [Demosthenes] xlii in the 320's, to the effect that
it was not easy to live off a property worth 4500 dr. ([Dem.] xlii 22).
His point, astonishing at first sight, is a just one if considered in
terms of a rentier's values. He would need a return of over 15% from
such a property if he were to have an income equivalent to that of a
contemporary skilled workman, 700 dr. a year or more (Jones 1957, 135 n.1),
and though such a return is perfectly possible the expenses of a
household or family of any size would require so much of his income
that to expect a man in such a position to be able to afford much
luxury, let alone even the most trivial civic liturgy, is obviously

quite out of the question. Even to quantify estates which were
'adequate, but not enough to perform liturgies' (Isaios xi 40) will,
on this evidence, involve going well above the 1 tal. mark. It
remains to consider whether, in the light of these figures and of
the general argument so far, certain other groups of men can be
identified as belonging to the propertied class. Five such groups
come into question. The first two are :
1) persons who are known to have owned property of a value well in
excess of 3 tal., or whose economic transactions presuppose such a
property level; and
2) persons known to have engaged in horse-rearing on a scale sufficient
to compete at Panhellenic Festivals.

The first group is self-explanatory. The few people whom it brings
in include, for example, Oionias of Atene, now known to have been one
of the richest Athenians of the fifth century (APF 11370), and Philippos
of Halai (APF p.537). The inclusion of the second group follows a
fortiori, from the clear indications (to be discussed below in Chapter VI)
that any man who could afford the money required for competitive horse-
breeding must already have been well inside the liturgical class:
correspondingly, the number of persons and families involved is much
smaller (see Appendix III).

Two further groups may also be considered together.
3) One consists of those men, about 75 of whom are known in all, whose
title to membership of the liturgical class consists only in that they
are attested as syntrierarchs at some date between 356 and 340. As
members of the trierarchic panel of 1200 under Periandros' law, some
at least of them will have been describable as 'poor' (πένητες), and

many of them will not have qualified for the trierarchical class
before 357 or after 340.

4) The other comprises about 70 men whose title consists only in
their being named on one of the diadikasia-documents ca. 380 . There
is some case, presented in Appendix I, for thinking that the persons
so named are not to be assigned to the narrow liturgical class but are,
instead, the owners of properties which, for whatever reason, were being
taken into, or dropped from, the schedule of the 1000 largest property-
units in Athens. As such, their title to inclusion in the Register is
much the same as that of the men in the first group.

The members of these two groups are included in the Register for
three reasons. The first is the doubt, in the case of any one particular
individual, whether his exclusion is justified: this doubt is particularly
strong, for example, with the men who are named as eponyms of naval
symmories, whom one would a priori expect to be among the richest members
of the symmories. Secondly, it would be useless to pretend that the
re-interpretation of the diadikasia-documents presented in Appendix I has
more than speculative value, so that the risk of unjustly denying
liturgical status to the persons mentioned theron is far from negligible.
Thirdly and conversely, even if the suggested reinterpretation is correct,
there is some value in making available a schedule of the persons who
are members only of these larger and less selective groups, so that the
position and prominence of them and of their families can be compared
with what is known of the smaller group of the liturgical class proper.

5) There remains a fifth group, the pentakosiomedimnoi. Since they
were created by Solon to be the office-holding class of the state,
prima facie they form just such an objectively-defined upper class as

this investigation seeks. However, there are acute difficulties involved, [which are sketched briefly at APF p.xxvi. It emerges that] the only men who can safely be placed in the Athenian upper class by virtue of pentakosiomedimnal status are the handful of sixth-century treasurers of Athene known from the two dedications $i^2 393 = $ LSAG 77 no.21 and $i^2 467 = $ DAA 330.

If those qualifying via membership of one of these five groups are included, the number of persons known or inferred as members of the Athenian propertied class during the three centuries from 600 to 300 is 779. The gross unevenness of their incidence through this period robs this figure of much significance, but a much clearer picture can be gained if this 300-year period is divided into nine conventional generations of 33 years each and if each of the persons who qualify for the Register is assigned to one (an.not more than one) of these generations. If this is done, a person being assigned to a particular generation if his liturgical activity or his high economic status is attested wholly or mainly in those 33 years, it is rational to hope that the totals so reached represent the number of men in each successive human generation whom we know to have occupied a position in the Athenian propertied class.

The evidence as thus divided is presented in Table 1 (see next page). It calls for several remarks.

1. Six of the fifteen men who qualify for the propertied class during the sixth century do so because of their chariot entries at Panhellenic Games, and come from four families. (Divided by generation, the men concerned are: Alkmeon (I) and Kallias (I); Miltiades (III) and Alkmeonides (I); Kimon (I) and Alkibiades (I). See Appendix III.)

32

Table 1

2 men attested during the years 600-566 (generation A)
10 "	"	"	"	"	566-544 (	"	B)
3 "	"	"	"	"	533-500 (	"	C)
16 "	"	"	"	"	500-466 (	"	D)
32 "	"	"	"	"	466-433 (	"	E)
71 "	"	"	"	"	433-400 (	"	F)
154 "	"	"	"	"	400-366 (	"	G)
334 "	"	"	"	"	366-333 (	"	H)
206 "	"	"	"	"	333-300 (	"	I)

Since at the end of the sixth century it was economically possible for
the liturgical system of financing to be instituted for the City
Dionysia, and similarly for the navy less than twenty years later, it
would be a major error to take these men as being in any sense representative of what was to become the liturgical class. That we know no others
is not an economic fact, but rather a political fact about a society which
produced little or no public documentation of its own and which was
analysed by later tradition more or (more likely) less satisfactorily in
terms of the political acts of a few wealthy and notable families.

2. Even though from generation D onwards the number of men attested in
each generation is sufficiently high to serve as a sample, the nature of
the selection cannot possibly be said to be random. On the whole, the
only men who are known to have performed agonistic liturgies are those
recorded on ii[2]2318 or on victor monuments, i.e. the competent or the
successful, while many of the men known from literary sources tend to be

those who engaged in litigation or those who as politicians or in some
other capacity were in the public eye. Only for the period from 377
till 322 does the evidence of the navy-lists provide a sample the
selection of which has not been influenced at source by extra-economic
considerations.

3.   Eighty-three of the men attested in generation G qualify only by
virtue of being listed on the diadikasia-documents (see APF Index I,
col.2). Seventy-five of those attested in generation H qualify only by
virtue of being listed as members of the Periandric 1200.

4.   The figures given above add up to 828, not 779, since many men are
attested in the upper class in more than one of these generations (for
details see APF p.xvii n.3). In addition, there are four men of whom it
is uncertain whether they should be placed in generation E or generation F;
13 men similarly 'floaters' as between generations G and H;   and 14 men
similarly 'floaters'as between generations H and I.

5.   If it be assumed (a) that the normal size of the liturgical class was
ca. 400 men at any one time in the fifth century, and ca. 300 men in the
fourth century, and (b) that property-units (as distinct from individual
items of property) changed hands mainly by inheritance and only once each
human generation, then each generation of the fifth century will have seen
ca. 800 men of a status to be attested in the liturgical class, and each
generation of the fourth century ca. 600 men. These figures are absolute
minima, since assumption (b) is plainly unsafe (see Chapter V). Yet even
of these minima the persons actually attested for the three generations of
the fifth century represent merely 2%, 4% and 9% respectively. For the
fourth-century, if the marginal persons identified in § 3 above are
excluded, the percentages for the three generations are distinctly higher,
nearly 12%, 43%, and 34.3% respectively. Yet it must be remembered that

these percentages are <u>maxima</u>, and would be greatly reduced if we had occasion to postulate any major instability in the composition of the propertied class, as there clearly was, for example, between 415 and 400 B.C.

iii

The argument of this chapter gives quantitative substance to the conclusion advanced in Chapter II, that it was only the members of the narrow liturgical class who really qualified to be described as 'rich'. It remains to place their economic position in its context, for the liturgical system of public financing was so stable and integral a part of the Athenian democratic constitution that it is reasonable to infer that the disproportionate burden which it imposed on the narrow liturgical class corresponded to an equally disproportionate distribution of property. Albeit with a very large margin of error, it is possible to construct a property-distribution graph for the fourth-century Athenian citizen population which shows this inference to be well-founded.

In constructing such a graph, there are four useful items of evidence.

(i) At any one time during the fourth century about 300 men, and not many more, had resources in excess of a figure between 3 and 4 <u>tal.</u> (see p. 22 above).

(ii) When the timocratic constitution was established in Athens in 321, 9000 men out of a total adult male citizen population of 21,000 owned property worth over 2000 dr. [24]

(iii)Only about 1200 men, or at the absolute maximum 2000, owned property of such a value, apparently about 1 <u>tal.</u> (p. 29 above) that from its

---

(24) Diod. xviii 18, 4-5; Plut.<u>Phok.</u> xxviii 7; Ktesikles ap.Athen. vi 272C.

income there was any perceptible surplus available which could be tapped
for the purposes of direct taxation. The figure of 1200 derives from
Periandros' law of 357 on the trierarchy. Demosthenes in 354 was indeed
prepared to suggest that the Periandric roster should be increased to
2000, so that when examptions were allowed for there would be a panel
of 1200 active men (Dem. xiv 16). He took for granted the economic
practicability of this proposal, and it is indeed true that even if the
graph is drawn in terms of the lower figure of 1200 the gradient of the
curve is already such that a very small reduction in the qualifying
level would bring in a large number of new properties: but his easy
assumption of the practicability of his proposal contrasts oddly with
his solicitous language of 330 (Dem. xviii 102-109), and from xiv 16-23
one receives the unfortunate impression that in 354 Demosthenes was thinking more in terms of arithmetical neatness and administrative convenience
than of individual circumstances and personal burdens.

(iv) In the fourth as in the fifth century, there were some fortunes
which were worth several or many times the minimum liturgical census.[25]
Their number at any one time was probably very small, and their stability
uncertain, but the construction of the graph should be such as to allow
for their incidence.

There are two other times of evidence which are at first sight
relevant but which cannot be used as primary evidence in this context.
(1) The first is the figure of 5740 or 6000 tal. attested as the timema
of Attika in and after 378/7 (Dem.xiv 19; Philochoros, FGH 328 F 46;
Polyb. ii 62, 7). Böckh's theory (1886, I 571 f) that this figure rep-

---

(25) E.G. those of Hipponikos (II): Kallias (II): Nikias (I): Oionias:
    Onetor (III): Demosthenes (I): Pasion: Epikrates: Euthykrates.

resents only a small fraction of the sum of the capital values of the
properties which were included in the assessment has been so repeatedly
refuted (cf. Beloch 1885, 237f: de Ste Croix 153, 36f: Thomsen 1964, 46f)
as to leave little reasonable doubt that it represents the integral of
the upper part of a property-distribution curve, but there is no
independent means at all of determining of how many property-units this
figure of 5750 or 6000 tal. is the sum. So far from this figure being of
use in constructing such a curve, it is only in terms of such a curve
that there is even the remotest chance of determining how many property-
units were included in the sum.

(2) Much the same is true for the obscure and disputed statement of
Pollux (viii 130) that the pentakosiomedimnoi 'used to spend a talent
on the state' (ἀνήλισκον εἰς τὸ δημόσιον τάλαντον) , the hippeis
similarly 3000 dr., the zeugitai 1000 dr., and the thetes nothing. That
these figures represent capitalizations of some kind for the Solonian
property-qualifications is, I think, an inescapable hypothesis, but we
have no real idea how many men in Athens were, e.g., hippeis or
pentakosiomedimnoi at any one time. The only available figures are minima
and therefore of limited demographic use. (A) There were 1000 cavalrymen
in the 420's (Ar. Knights 225) and the fourth century (Xen. Hipparch. ix 3),
but it cannot be assumed that they and only they are 'those assessed in
the class of hippeis' (οἱ τὴν ἱππάδα τελοῦντες) , for the language of
Isaios vii 39 and of Dionysios' hypothesis to Lys. xxxiv distinctly
implies the contrary. (B) Since the three boards of treasurers (tamiai
of Athene, tamiai of the Other Gods, and Hellenotamiai) were selected from
the pentakosiomedimnoi (Ath.Pol. viii I and xlvii I, and ML 58, lines
13-15, for the two sacred boards: assumed for the Hellenotamiai), and
since the holding of a second treasurership, whether on the same board

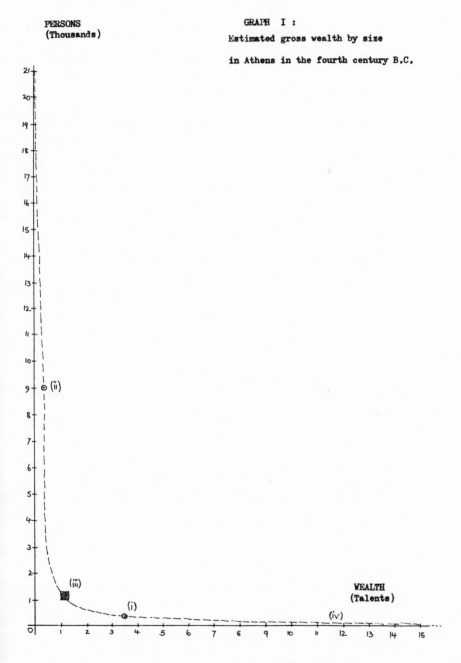

PERSONS
(Thousands)

GRAPH I :
Estimated gross wealth by size
in Athens in the fourth century B.C.

WEALTH
(Talents)

or another, is not attested and may have been illegal, at least 20 men
of pentakosiomedimnal status, or 30 in the late fifth century, should
have reached office-holding age every year: but at least 15 boards
are known to have less than their full complement of 10 men, and only
11 boards to have been fully manned, so that even these figures as a
basis for argument are unreliable. Hence the figures given by Pollux
are not in themselves of any practical use: they too gain significance
only in terms of a distribution-curve constructed from other data.

Graph I is therefore constructed on the basis of the four items
of evidence quoted above. That it is tentative and approximate hardly
needs pointing out, but with this caveat it can be offered as what is
likely to be a reasonably accurate representation of the distribution
of property among the members of the Athenian citizen body in the
fourth century B.C. Moreover, I doubt if the general pattern was very
different in the fifth century. It is true that the citizen body was
larger, being certainly not less than 30,000 for much of the century,[26]
but the distension thereby involved in the graph is probably cancelled
out by the existence of a somewhat larger and richer liturgical class.
A major difference in the distribution-pattern between the fifth and
fourth centuries can be taken as unlikely.

---

(26) Gomme 1933, 26 Table I: Jones 1957, 161f: Meiggs 1964.

Chapter IV

THE SOURCES OF WEALTH

The available information on this subject is such that it is
impossible to take evidence which applies only to, or to make statements which are true only of, the Athenian propertied class as
defined in chapter III. Nevertheless, partly because much of the
evidence does concern this class and partly because the economic
potentialities of its members formed so disproportionately large a
part of the total economic potential of Athens, it is rational to
expect not only that such patterns and changes as can be observed
should apply at least as much to that class as to any other, but also
that the kinds of activity which are known to have placed men in that
class are paralleled for other men both in the class and below it.

The kind of definition given by Solon in 580 to his new property-
classes[1] implies that in the early sixth century in Athens productive
wealth which could not be measured in terms of agricultural produce was
politically negligible. This is the only indication there is of the
sources of wealth available to Athenians at the time, but it is
sufficient to pose a sharp contrast with the more developed economy of
the fourth and late fifth centuries. However, its implications are not
to be misunderstood. In the first place, it cannot be taken to exclude
ownership of domestic and agricultural slaves on the Homeric model[2]

---

(1) Ath.Pol. vii 3; Plut. Solon xviii 1-2. For the date see Hignett 1952, 316f.

(2) Cf. ᾳ 398; λ 735f.; η 103; ξ 115 and 399; χ 421f.; ω 210, 365f., and 389f.

or to exclude the possession of bullion, in artefacts or (later on)
in coin, on the hoarding pattern familiar from Homer to the fourth
century and beyond and spectacularly exemplified by known coin-hoards.[3]
In the second place, it does not necessarily mean that other sources
of wealth were economically negligible. Though it is very easy to
over-estimate the numerical and economic importance of Athenian
merchants, the possibility cannot be excluded that there were men in
Athens in 580 who had made mercantile profits in the same way, though
not on the same scale, as Kolaios of Samos had done ca. 638 (Hdt. iv
152, 1-4). Yet, as Cook (1959, 116) rightly pointed out, it cannot be
assumed a priori that Athenian pottery was exported in Athenian ships.
On the contrary, the distribution of Attic Bf. ware in the sixth century
is such as to create the presumption that it was carried on Korinthian
ships, at least initially (cf. Bailey 1940), and whatever be the truth
underlying the tradition of Solon's currency reform (Ath.Pol. x 1-2 ;
Plut. Solon xv 2-4), the fact that Athens' first coins were didrachms
equivalent in weight to the Korinthian stater of 8.6 or 8.7 gr. points
very much the same way. The tradition that Solon himself was a merchant
at one stage (Ath.Pol. xi 1; Plut. Solon ii 1) is not in itself incredible
but cannot safely be generalized.

---

(3) Cf. Z 288-289; β 337f.; o 99f.; φ 8f. Money ἐνλον : Antiphon, DK⁵
    87 [80] B54; Dem. xxvii 10 and 53; Dem. xxix 46f.; Isaios xi 43.
    Cf. the hoarding motif which presumably or certainly underlies no
    less than seven comedies entitled Thesauros (of Krates, Anaxandrides,
    Philemon, Diphilos, Archedikos, Menandros, and Dioxippos). For the
    physical evidence of coin hoards see Thompson-Mørkholm-Kraay 1973.

Again, there is a strong case for at least the <u>de facto</u> inalienability of land by private treaty in Attika in the archaic period. The legal question can be left on one side, for the evidence suggests that economically it made very little difference whether the sanctions against releasing land were legal or not. The explicit tradition that before Solon's reforms loans were made on the security of the body (<u>Ath.Pol.</u> ii 2), must imply <u>either</u> that this was the only possible form of security, land being legally inalienable, <u>or</u> that this was the only acceptable form of security, being the only form the consequences of which would leave unimpaired the productive capacity of the land owned by the family of the debtor. Either way, the result is the same - a strong sanction against releasing land. Similarly, though a law of Solon reported by Aristotle (<u>Pol.</u> 1266b 17) clearly envisages - because it restricts - the possibility of acquiring land, his definition of his property-classes wielded an effective sanction against selling: a man who parted with land ran the very real risk of dropping a rung in the class-ladder and thereby having his possibilities of holding office sharply restricted. For practical purposes this was enough; no man would sell if he could possibly help it.

Furthermore, it is hard to envisage a mechanism whereby trading profits could be easily converted into the kind of property-holding - agricultural land - which Solon's qualification-criteria placed at a political preumium. The only real possibility is <u>via</u> the public sale of confiscated land, but the historicity of the one recorded example of this practice in the sixth century, Kallias' purchase of the property of the exiled Peisistratos (Hdt. vi 121, 2) is not beyond question (see <u>APF 7826</u>, § 2). The net effect of these arguments is to compel the assumption either

that merchants were apolitical quietists or (more likely) that
mercantile trading was practically insignificant as an avenue for
social and economic advancement.

Thereafter there is no appreciable first-hand evidence for well
over a century. When, as for the generation that lived through the
Peloponnesian War, it again becomes possible to attempt a description
of the sources of wealth available to the inhabitants of Attika, the
striking transformation which is immediately perceptible can be
traced directly to the development of new sources of personal wealth.
Some five such sources are worth characterizing in detail.
(1) Probably the first in importance is industrial slavery in workships
and in the silver-mines. The prevalence of this can partly be gauged
by considering how many men of economic or political importance in the
fifth century are known to have derived some or all of their wealth from
the ownership of industrial slaves. Those attested, in approximate chronological order, are: Sophokles' father Sophillos of Kolonos, owner of
slave bronze-smiths or carpenters;[4] Kleainetos and his son Kleon of
Kydathenaion, successively owners of a tannery (APF 8674); Hipponikos

---

(4) Vit.Soph. i, explicitly correcting the statements of Aristoxenos (F115
  Wehrli) that Sophillos was himself a bronze-smith or carpenter, and of
  Istros (FGH 334 F33) that he was a dagger-maker. The biographer's corr-
  ection is entirely a priori, though no doubt correct in substance. For
  Sophokles there was a motive for the correction, that of rescuing a poet
  from the libel of low origins: other politicians were not so fortunate.

of Alopeke, owner of 600 slaves leased out on contract in the silver-

mines (APF 7826 7); Philemoniedes, owner of 300 slaves similarly

employed (APF p.535); Isokrates' father Theodoros of Erchia, owner of

a workshop of slave flute-makers (APF 7716); Lysikles, variously

described as a sheep-dealer and as a cobbler;[5] Kleippides of Acharnai

and his sons Kleophon and Philinos, with all of whom it is now

plausible to connect the 1y re-making business attested for Kleophon;[6]

Nikias of Kydantidai, owner of 1000 slaves leased out on contract in

the silver-mines (APF 10808); Eukrates of Melite, the oakum-dealer;[7]

Hyperbolos of Perithoidai, the lamp-maker (PA 13910); Anthemion of

Euonymon and his son Anytos, successively owners of a tannery (APF 1324);

and Kephalos of Syracuse and his sons Lysias and Polemarchos, success-

ively owners of a shield-factory emplying up to 120 slaves (APF C9).

Not surprisingly, the same is true for the fourth century.

We know of: Kephalos of Kollytos, whose father was a potter (schol.Ar.

Ekkl. 253); Nausikydes of Cholargos, miller and corn-dealer (APF 8443);

Antisthenes of Kytherros, slave-owner and successful business man (APF 1194);

Iasos of Kollytos, the stone-mason who became a choregos (APF 7423);

Aischines of Sphettos, who started an unguent-factory but found himself

in serious financial trouble (Lysias F1 Thal.); Timomachos of Acharnai,

the carpenter whose descendant was a general and married into Kallistratos'

family (APF 8157, IV); Keramon, grown wealthy from industrial slave-

_____

(5) Plut. Per. xxiv 6; Schol. Ar. Knights 739 and 740.

(6) And. i 146; Aisch. ii 76; Ath.Pol. xxviii 3; schol. Ar. Thesm. 805;

schol. Ar.Frogs 681; E. Vanderpool, Hesperia 21 (1952) 114f;

A.E. Raubitschek, Hesperia 23 (1954) 68f.

(7) Ar. Knights 129 with schol.; Ar. F 696, I 562 K; Kratinos F 295,

Γ 98 K.

owning (Xen.Mem. ii 7, 3-4); Kyrebos, owner of a bakery (Xen. Mem. ii 7,6); Demeas of Kollytos and Menon, each owners of cloak-making businesses (ibid); Arizelos of Sphettos, owner of two work-shops in the silver mines and of a shoe-making business with 9 or 10 slaves (Aisch. i 97 and 101); Pasion, later of Acharnai, owner of a large shield-factory (APF 11672, VI-VII); the elder Demosthenes of Paiania, owner of 32 or 33 knife-makers and of 20 bed-makers (APF 3597, XIII); Pantainetos, owner of a workshop in the silver-mines employing 30 slaves (Dem. xxxvii 4); and Leokrates, owner of a workshop of bronzesmiths (Lyk. Leokr. 23 and 58). The list could be lengthened by the inclusion of those who are known to have had only a few industrial slaves, but its size is already sufficient indication of the prevalence of industrial slave labour. The owners include aristocrats such as Hipponikos and many leitourgountes such as Kleainetos, Hyperbolos, Theodoros, and Nikias from the fifth century, or Nausikydes, Antisthenes, Iasos and Pasion from the fourth, as well as men of whom all we are entitled to say is that industrial slavery as a source of income gave them sufficient return either simply to enjoy the leisure of rentier status or to allow them to give ambition its scope and engage in full-time political activity. It should not now need re-emphasizing that the public men of the late fifth century who encounter-ed animadversions in Comedy for their trading or craftsmen backgrounds were rentiers, and not working with their own hands (αὐτουργοί), by the time they began to appear in the public eye: just as 'Euphronios would remain ὁ κεραμεύς even after he had ceased to fashion vases on the wheel' (Beazley 1946, 26), so too they remained tanners or lyre-makers no matter what their wealth. Indeed, Anytos, Kleon, Kephalos, and probably Kleippides

and Nikias were second-generation men with a natural path to public
life provided by a fortune built up by their fathers from industrial
slavery: but for his physical disability exactly the same would most
likely have been true for Isokrates, and for Lysias too had he obtained
Athenian citizenship after 403. I would imagine that this was the
normal pattern for families with an industrial background (it was
followed in the fourth century by Apollodoros, Timarchos, and Demosthenes),
but it is quite likely that there were men who began as αὐτουργοί
and made money quickly enough to transfer to public life in their own
persons rather than in their sons': Antisthenes seems to have been one
such, and so perhaps was Hyperbolos.

    This kind of background was not altogether new in the fifth century.
From the late sixth century onwards potters had been growing rich enough
from their craft to commission Akropolis dedications from sculptors such
as Endoios and Antenor.[8] Yet so far as one can judge from the
admittedly shaky evidence provided by pictorial representations of
potters' workshops[9] and by calculations of the total number of men
active in producing painted pottery at any one time,[10] the average
number of men employed in a potters' workshop was at most five, and this

---

(8) DAA 46 no. 44; 213 no. 178; 232 no. 197; 255 no. 225. Less certain
    examples are listed by Beazley 1946, 23 note 1.

(9) Glotz 1926, 140 fig. 22 (a potter and seven men) and 205 fig 26 (a
    potter and four men); Beazley 1946, pl. 1, 1 (potter and two men);
    G.M.A. Richter, The Craft of Athenian Pottery (New Haven, 1923) 66
    fig.60 (potter and two men), 71 fig. 66 (three men and a woman), and 74
    fig 70 (three men).

(10) Cook 1959, 118f. suggested that in the fifth century there may have
    been about 125 painters producing Rf. ware at any one time, and about
    400-500 men employed in the trade at any one time.

is part of the point: what does seem to have been new in the fifth century is the scale on which industrial slaves were used and the crafts in which they were employed. In the first place, the making and selling of many goods on a scale large enough to justify the help of slave labour presupposes a retail market of a kind quite out of the question in the early sixth century or before the developed every-day use of small-denomination coinage (Kraay 1964). In the second place, the industry in which slaves are known to have been employed on the largest scale is precisely the one industry for the development of which a _terminus ante quem non_ is available. The analysis by neutron activation of Wappenmunzen and early owls carried out by Kraay and Emeleus (1962) suggests that the silver used in the coining of the Wappenmünzen came from sources outside Attika, probably from Thrace, and that it was only from the 520's onwards that home-produced silver from Laureion began to be used for Athenian coins. _Ca._ 520 can reasonably be taken as the earliest date for the employment of slaves in any numbers at Laureion, and 483 as the earliest date for their employment on the scale indicated by Xenophon.

All this bears out the view that the growth of industrial slavery should not be pre-dated:[11] indeed I would be inclined to suppose that it was in fact a largely fifth-century, and a largely Athenian, phenomenon. Such other evidence as there is points the same way. (a) The scale of Korinthian painted pottery production is said to have been such that the industry cannot have employed even half of the working force of 500 suggested for fifth century Athens (Cook 1959, 121) and if the law against slave-owing ascribed to Periandros

---

(11) 'During the seventh century': Glotz 1926, 71f. 'Well under way
    before 600 B.C.': Westermann 1955, 3.

(Nikolaos, FGH 90 F 58) is genuine, it follows analogously that
industrial slavery at Korinth even at the time of her ceramic
supremacy was not an indispensable part of her economy. (b) The
tradition that the Chians were the first to use bought slaves
(χρυσωνητοί)[12] has been connected with the metallurgical developments associated with Glaukos of Chios[13] in the early seventh
century, but this in itself cannot have involved the employment of
slaves on a very large scale. The comparatively large number of
slaves attested for Chios in 412 (Thuc. viii 40,2) is more likely to
reflect the growth of a rationally organized agriculture producing the
wine and figs for which the island was famous,[14] and consistently
enough Thucydides gives the impression that the island's prosperity
in 412 consisted in its land, 'beautifully furnished' and unharmed
since 480 (Thuc. viii 24, 3-4), rather than in the scale of its craftsman industry. (c) The statements of Hekataios and Timaios that the
Greeks used not to possess bought slaves as servants [15] clearly, from

---

(12) Theopompos, FGH 115 F 122; Poseidonios, FGH 87 F 38.

(13) Hdt. i 125, 2; Westermann (note 39) 4.

(14) For references see Burchner, RE 3 (1899) 2291 and 2293f.

(15) Hekataios, FGH 1 F 127 = Hdt. vi 137, 3; Timaios, FGH 566 F 11.

their contexts, apply to household chattel slavery [16] and imply
nothing either way about industrial slavery. Possibly of more
relevance is the widespread use in Old Comedy of the motif of the
slaveless Golden Age, [17] for *prima facie* it looks as if it might be a
reaction to something of contemporary importance, but the lack of need
for slaves is presented as a consequence of the effortlessness of food
production in the ideal human condition rather than as an essential
part of that ideal.

There are three ways of assessing the prevalence of industrial and
craftsman slavery, (a) The Attic Stelai [18] record the sale of some 53
slaves in 414. Of these 40 are given no occupation and were therefore
presumably domestic; of seven (Stele XI, lines 3ff) it is uncertain
whether they had any occupation or not; and only six are given an

---

(16) This is clear from Timaios' use of the word Διᾱκονεῖν and from
the nature of the protests of those whom Mnason's innovations threw
into unemployment. Since Timaios says that this kind of slavery
was contrary to codified custom in Lokris and Phokis, it is worth
hazarding the suggestion that Periandros' law (Nikolaos FGH 90 F 58)
was directed not against industrial slavery but against household
slavery of the kind which was new in Central Greece in the fourth
century - and for what it is worth there is evidence from another
context that Periandros was concerned to maintain full employment
(Ar. Pol. 1313 b 24-25).

(17) Kratinos F 165, I 64 K; Krates F 14, I 133 K; Pherekrates F 130,
I 182 K.

(18) Hesperia 22 (1953) 240f. and Hesperia 30 (1961) 23f.

occupation of any kind (and one of these six, the Τραπεζοποιός , was really a domestic).[19] (b) We know the names of 148 men, almost all active in the fourth century, who were financially involved in the workings of the silver mines as operators (lessees and registrants) or as owners of ergasteria),[20] and therefore must have employed slave labour.   Of these men 47 are certainly identifiable, and another three doubtfully, as men who have merited entry in APF either directly or indirectly: i.e. just under a third of known mining entrepreneurs qualify in some way as members of the propertied class. (c) The manumission lists[21] record the manumissions of 171 slaves whose trade or activity is preserved. Of these, the largest single category comprises domestic slaves (72 in all, of whom 50 are talasiourgoi ('wool-spinners' or 'spinsters') and another 17 children). The next largest category is retailing, with 36, followed by 28 craftsmen (shoemakers, gold-smiths, tanners, etc.), 13 in agriculture, six in service-trades (barbers, seamstress, etc.), four in transport and 12 miscellaneous or uncertain. Given that no mining slave is recorded (the one possible instance was emend-ed away by Lewis 1959, 231), and that these records will relate only to

---

(19) Stele II, line 73:   see W.K. Pritchett, Hesperia 25 (1956) 279. The
       others are: a mule-driver, a goldsmith, a skewermaker and two shoemakers.
(20) See the indices drawn up by M. Crosby, Hesperia 19 (1950) 298f. and 26
       (1957) 21f. This figure excludes men attested merely as property-owners.
(21) ii² 1553-1578, as re-edited with additions by Lewis 1959 and Lewis 1968.
       The figures given by Gomme 1933, 41ff, are now superseded.

slaves able to raise the 100 dr. required for the dedication of the phiale recorded at the end of each entry on these documents, these figures are more likely to underrepresent than to overrepresent the prevalence of craftsman and non-domestic slavery in the Athens of the 320's.

(2) Right from the beginning of contemporary documentation rents from houses and farmland appear as a common constituent of the income of a man of any substance.[22] Two of the proximate causes of this are fairly clear.

(i) By 431 the number of (adult male) metics resident in Attika was well above 3000 (Thuc.ii 31,2 : Gomme 1933,5) and was more likely comparable to, or even greater than, the 10,000 who were living in Attika at the end of the fourth century.[23] Metics had to live and work somewhere. Since

---

(22) For metropolitan Athens cf. the sources quoted in note 30 below and Isaios viii 35. The strict provisions against indiscriminate leasing laid down (whatever the exact restorations may be) in the Salamis decree (ML 14, lines 3f.) imply that leasing was already current practice at the end of the sixth century, but since absentee land-lordism is more likely in an overseas property and more of a danger in a militarily exposed zone such as Salamis very likely was at the time (H.T. Wade-Gery, CQ 40 [1946] 103), there may be dangers in generalizing the implication too readily.

(23) Ktesikles ap. Athen. vi 272 C (Demetrios' census). See Gomme 1933, 26 Table I; id. HCT II 36f.; Jones 1957, 165; (Whitehead 1977, 97f.).

they could not normally own real property in Attika they had to occupy

accommodation provided for them (at a profit) by Athenian citizens;

and to their number can be added an unknown number of citizen families

who, coming from country demes to the City or Peiraieus in the sixth

and fifth centuries, may not have wished, or not been able, to buy a

house. The latter point deserves expansion. Quite apart from the

problem of assessing the legality of land purchase before the late fifth

century, houses were expensive. The cheapest house-price recorded is

105 dr. (Hesperia 22 [1953] 287 Stele X line 15), and this was in 414 for

a house in a deme (Semachidai) uncomfortably near Dekeleia. Ca. 360

even a cottage cost getting on for 300 dr.(Isaios ii 35), and most

preserved house-prices are well over 1000 dr. (see the full list in Pritchett

1956, 270f.). For a man escaping with his family to Athens from rural

poverty and under-employment in Attika or the islands, such prices were

quite out of the question.

The consequence is worth following up in detail. It is a cliché

that most metics were engaged in craftsman industry or in trade (see

Whitehead 1977, 116 ff). Gerhardt's figures (Gerhardt 1933, 21) for

metics known from epigraphical sources are: 39.9% engaged in craftsman

industry and another 8.5% as industrial entrepreneurs, 20.9% in merchant-

ing and retail trade, 12.4% women in employment, 9.8% miscellaneous, and

only 8.5% in agriculture. Some qualifications do need to be made. These

and Clerc's figures (below) include the freedmen and freedwomen attested

on the manumission documents, who cannot automatically be assumed to be

becoming a representative sample of the metic population. Also, Gerhardt

(1933, 20) rightly pointed out that metics engaged in the liberal arts

should not be forgotten, and since epigraphical sources will have had much less occasion to note the existence of such people, the evidence may underrate their numbers. However, the correction factor is unlikely to be large.

Correspondingly, most metics lived in urban or suburban demes (see references in Whitehead 1977, 100 n.31). Clerc's figures (Clerc 1893, 450f) for known metic demotics are:- Melite 50, Peiraieus 41, Kollytos and Alopeke 26 each, Kydathenaion 22, Skambonidai 18, Keiriadai 9, and no other deme more than 6: antiquated though these figures are, the distribution-pattern they suggest is still accurate enough. It looks very much as if behind these figures there lies a major housing boom in speculative building during the fifth century. In the first place, there are now several excavated examples of fifth-century building in and around Athens on sites previously farmland or sparsely inhabited,[24] and this even aside from the deliberate planning and development of Peiraieus. In the second place there was the development of the synoikia, or multiple-dwelling: attested from the 420's onwards [25] and - since this is principally a fact about our sources - no doubt existing well before then (and not only in Athens: cf. those attested at Kerkyra in 427 by Thucydides iii

---

(24)   See the reference ap. J.E. Jones, L.H. Sackett, and A.J. Graham, BSA 57 (1962) 102 note 30. I see no means of deciding whether the figure of 10,000 houses given by Xenophon (Mem.iii 6,14) applies to the Asty or to the whole of Attika, so it is best left out of account.

(25)   Ar.Knights 1001;   Xen. Ath.Pol. i 18;   Ar. Georgoi F 115, I 420 K; Hesperia 22 (1953) 263 Stele IV, line 11;   Ar. Thesm. 273;   Isaios ii 27 and xi 44; Dem. xxxvi 3 and 34-35; Dem. xxxviii 7;   Aisch. i 43 and 124-125. See Böckh 1886, I 83f. and 177, and Pritchett 1956, 268.

74, 2), they represented a very considerable investment[26] but could
evidently be exceedingly profitable (Athen. xii 542F). Clearly, no
small number of well-off Athenian citizens in the fifth and fourth
centuries owed part of their incomes to urban landlordism on a considerable scale.

(ii) On the whole, Athenian landowners were not latifondisti, and large
unitary landed estates of any size were very exceptional. True, there
is a case for supposing that at the end of the sixth century the various
branches of the Alkmeonidai held between them a large belt of agricultural
land in the three adjoining demes Alopeke, Agryle, and Xypete south of
Athens (see APF 9688, XIV), but otherwise the two biggest known estates,
owned by Alkibiades (Plato Alkib 123c) and Aristophanes son of Nikophemos
(Lys.xix 29: APF 5951), are of rather under, and rather over, 300 plethra
respectively (i.e. 2.85 sq.km), the latter being worth over 4 tal. 1000 dr.
(Lys. xix 42). There is, it is true, Phainippos' estate at Kytheros,
"40 stades in circumference" ([Dem.] xlii 5) (see APF 14734), but since
the persiflage involved in that figure has been exposed by De Ste Croix
1966, 109ff., Phainippos' estate cannot safely be cited as a third very
large unitary holding. The paucity of such references is probably not
chance, for it appears to have been far more usual for a man of property
to own many small estates or properties scattered throughout Attika.

---

(26) Known prices are: 1600 dr. ([Dem.] liii 13), 2000 dr. (Isaios
viii 35), at least 2000 dr. (Dem. xxix 3 plus Dem. xxi 1), at least
$3705\frac{1}{2}$ dr. (Hesperia 5 [1936] 393 no.10, lines 118-152), 4000 dr.
(Isaios v 26-27), 4400 dr. (Isaios vi 19-21 and 33), 5000 dr.(Isaios
v 29), 5000 dr. (Lysias xix 29), and 10,000 dr. (Dem. xlv 28).

For example, Euphiletos of Kydathenaion, who was convicted for both mutilation and profanation in 415/4, owned a house the position of which is lost, a house in Semachidai, a piece of land in Gargettos, a piece of land, a garden, and a house, all in Myrrhinoutta, and a piece of land in Aphidna.[27] Pherekles of Themakos, similarly convicted on both counts in 415/4, owned a house and a piece of land in Bate, a piece of land π[α]ρὰ Λκν[- - -] , a piece of land by the Pythion, a house-site by the Pythion, a piece of land by the Herakleion, and a tract of mountainous scrub-land (ὀργάς)in or near Kykale,[28] as well as the house in Themakos known from Andokides (i 17). Adeimantos of Skambonidai, convicted for profanation in 415/4, owned farmland together with a house at ΐ[- - -] on Thasos, possibly (though he may not be the owner) an oak coppice, pine grove and a house in [- - -] , some land at Ophryneion in the Troad, and a piece of land in Xypete.[29] In the 390's Dikaiogenes III of Kydathenaion owned a house in the City with a garden adjoining, two cottages outside the city wall, 60 _plethra_ of agricultural land in the Plain, a bath-house, and a tenement-house in Kerameikos (Isaios v ii, 22, and 26: APF 3773). In the 370's Euktemon of Kephisia owned a tenement-house in Kerameikos and another in Peiraieus, a house in the City, a farm at Athmonon, a bath-house at Serangeion in Mounychia, and a piece of land of unspecified location (Isaios vi 19-20, 23, and 33. APF 15164).

---

(27) _Hesperia_ 22 (1953) 268 Stele VI, line 89, and ibid. 287 Stele X, lines 15-18.

(28) _Hesperia_ 22 (1953) 268 Stele VI, lines 93-106, with new restorations by D.M. Lewis. For the topographical and other problems presented by the mention of the ὀργάς , see Pritchett 1956, 267.

(29) _Hesperia_ 22 (1953) 268 Stele VI, lines 55f.; _ibid._ 287 Stele X, lines 1-2 and 11; _Hesperia_ 30(1961) 25 Stele II, lines 5-6.

At his death in 370/69 Pasion of Acharnai owned real property in three
demes, including two tenement-houses, farmland in Pelekes or Acharnai,
and perhaps the premises of the bank in Peiraieus (APF 11672, V). In
the 360's Arizelos of Sphettos owned a City house, a tract of scrub-land
at Sphettos, a piece of land at Alopeke and another at Kephisia, a farm
at Kephisia, and two workshops in the mining area (Aisch. i 97 and 101).
Also in the 360's Stratokles of Oion had a farm at Thria, a house in Melite
and another house at Eleusis, and his brother Theopompos of Oion had a piece
of land in Oinoe and another at Prospalta together with a house in the
City (Isaios xi 37ff: APF 2921, XIV). At the time of his exile in 343/2
Philokrates of Hagnous owned a piece of land and a house in Hagnous, three
pieces of land whose location is lost, some scrub-land in Hagnous, and
some other property (specification lost) in Hagnous, two workshops in
Melite and two houses in Melite (Hesperia 5 (1936) 393 no.10, lines 15f.
and 105f.).

These examples should be enough to show how widespread this pattern
of property-ownership was. Since it was clearly quite impracticable for
thw owner of such widely scattered and fragmented property-holdings to
cultivate them properly through the direct labour of his own household, the
obvious and necessary solution was to lease individual components out to
tenant-farmers in a manner which is, indeed, adequately attested throughout
the fourth and late fifth-centuries.[30] Now it is of course true that the

---

(30) Kratinos, Ploutoi (GLP I 196 no. 38(b), line 33); Hesperia 22 (1953)
249 Stele II, lines 173-175; ibid. 268 Stele VI, lines 64-73 and
110-115; Xen. Mem. ii 7, 2 and iii 11, 4; Xen. Symp. viii 25; Lys.
vii 4 and 9-10; Tod, GHI II 100, lines 10,15, 17, 20, 22, and 25;
Isaios xi 42; Theoph. Char. iv 5. See Jones 1957, 139 note 62, and
p. 49 above.

pre-Solonic hektemoroi were functionally, though not legally, in much
the same position as the fourth-century tenant farmer, but even apart
from the difference in legal context, there is an important distinction.
Rents paid in kind (as under the hektemorage system) were hardly if at
all convertible to use in a non-agricultural milieu, while the fifth-
and fourth-century rents were almost universally paid and reckoned in
coin [31] and were therefore immediately available for a multiplicity of
kinds of economic or political re-investment. The value of such a facility
to the landlord needs no stressing.

(3) The third new source of wealth which is worth singling out for special
attention is the ownership of, leasing of, or money-lending on the security
of, property outside Attika by Athenian nationals. The importance of this
practice during the fifth century can be judged partly by direct evidence
(see below), partly from the fact that Andokides in 391 was aware that
"the recovery of Chersonese, of our colonies, and of our overseas possessions
and debts" was widely regarded in Athens as a good reason for continuing the
war, [32] and partly from the well-known fact that in his manifesto of Spring
377, in order to make renewed Athenian hegemony acceptable, Aristoteles felt
it necessary to cancel existing property-owning by Athenians publicly or

---

(31) Lys. xxxii 15 is the only exception, a rent of a property in
Chersonese being paid in corn in the last decade of the fifth century.

(32) And. iii 15. His word for "overseas possessions", ἐγκτήματα,
echoes the legal word ἔγκτησις and makes it clear that he was
thinking of private property outside Attika at least as much as of
property held under public auspices (as in a klerouchy). Aristoteles'
decree (see next note) similarly uses the same word for both publicly
and privately owned property (lines 27-28).

privately in the territory of any state in the Second Confederacy and to prohibit it and mortgage-transactions henceforward.[33]

Property in this category falls into four groups: (a) land occupied by Athenian citizens and others in Athenian colonies; (b) land owned by an Athenian god or goddess (τεμένη) and leased out to Athenian citizens or metics or to local men; (c) land assigned to Athenian citizens in Athenian klerouchies; and (d) property overseas which passed into the possession of an Athenian citizen by private treaty (purchase) or inheritance.

The full analysis of Athenian property-holding over-seas and of the juridical and political problems associated with it is too complex to be undertaken here. It is also the less relevant, in that what matters in the present context is not so much the genesis and development of Athenian public policy as the effect of public policy on the opportunities available to Athenian citizens and the extent to which these opportunities were taken. Moreover, there is a further limitation: since one case (Brea) is certainly known where participation in a colony was restricted to members of the two lowest property-classes, thetes and zeugites (ML 49, lines 40-1), and since there is a good case for thinking that at least part of the intention and the effect of klerouchies was to resettle thetes and thereby to increase the size of the hoplite class,[34] these developments affect the position of the Athenian propertied class only if it is demonstrable (a) that men were living in Attika while drawing revenues from overseas properties as absentee

---

(33) ii²43 = Tod, GHI II 123, lines 25-31 and 35-46; Diod. xv 29, 8.

(34) See Jones 1957, 168-9 (arguing from the Brea decree itself and Thuc. iii 50, 2). For the basic political idea cf. the proposal 'to turn the thetes into hoplites' (τοὺς θῆτας ὁπλίσαι) (Antiphon F 61 Blass, with K.J. Dover, CQ 44 [1950] 55).

landlords, and (b) that poor men ceased to be the only men concerned
or that those concerned ceased to be poor men. Both are indeed demonstrably the case, but these conditions are sufficient to exclude from
further consideration colonies such as Ennea Hodoi, Brea, Amphipolis,
Lemnos, Imbros, or Skyros, or the early klerouchy of 506 to Chalkis.

Nevertheless, what remains in groups (b) and (d) is quite considerable. Group (b) (_temene_ of Athenian deities) needs little attention
here, for though evidence for such _temene_ is not scanty[35] the leasing
to individuals of such _temene_ for revenue-earning purposes is much less
well attested. All that is known is (a) the leasing of property on
Kythnos and at Styra in Euboia belonging to the Eleusinian sanctuary,[36]

---

(35) For the fifth-century boundary-stones of _temene_ of Athene, Ion,
and the Eponymoi on Samos, see Barron 1964, 35f.; on Kos, Paton
and Hicks 160 no. 148 (temenos of Athene) (Barron 1964, 43); on
Aigina, _IG_ IV 29-32 (_temenos_ of Athene) and _IG_ IV 33-38 (temenos
of Apollo Poseidon) (Barron 1964, 44); at Brea, ML 49, lines 10-11
(deity not specified); on Lesbos in 427, Thuc. iii 50, 2 (300
out of 3000 set aside for the gods); on Lemnos, _SEG_ III 117 (_temenos_
of the tribe Antiochis, attested in 303/2). See Kahrstedt, 1934, 32f.

(36) i^{2}313, line 147; i^{2}318 = _Hesperia_ 12 (1943) 34 no.7 = _SEG_ X 211.

and (b) the leasing of property on Euboia, described as [ca.5]c τεμένε
at Chalkis, Hestiaia (Orobiai), Eretria, Posideion, and And[- -].[37]

    The known evidence for private property-holding outside Attika and
Salamis (group (d)) is now as follows. (i) Thucydides of Halimous
owned the mineral rights of gold-mines in Thrace in the 420's (Thuc. iv
105, 1). No doubt this facility was wholly exceptional and due to his
family links with the area (APF 7268), but it should be remembered that
he was probably not unique in having this kind of connexion. In spite of
Perikles' citizenship law of 451/0, there must have been a far from
negligible number of people in late fifth-century Athens who were in a
position to inherit property outside Attika from non-Athenian relatives
on the distaff side, and the right of intermarriage (ἐπιγαμία) with
Euboia attested by Lysias xxxiv 3 should have allowed this to continue.
(ii) The family of Euthyphron of Prospalta had a farm on Naxos before 404
and employed a 'serf' (πελάτης)as a labourer on it (Plato, Euthyphron
4c). Since the family was well enough off even after 404 to employ him
and several other slave domestics, this farm on Naxos, even if it was part
of the klerouchy (and this is not stated or implied), cannot have been the
only or even the major component of the family's estates. (iii) A certain
Eutheros had lived till 405 on his property overseas (Xen.Mem. ii 8,1).
Since he had no inherited property in Attika and was working as a hired
labourer after 404, it is likely enough that he had been a klerouch, though
this is not stated. (iv) Several of the men convicted in 415/4 owned or
were working property outside Attika. One man (unidentifiable) was working,

---

(37) i²376 = Hesperia 12 (1943) 28 no.6 = SEG X 304.

but not necessarily the owner of, an estate at Eretria,[38] and an
estate at Eretria is mentioned elsewhere;[39] (v) Oionias of Atene
owned agricultural property in the Lelantine Plain and at Diros and
Geraistos on Euboia worth no less than 81 tal. 2000 dr.;[40] (vi) Nikides
of Melite owned what appears to have been agricultural property at Diros
on Euboia;[41] (vii) Adeimantos of Skambonidai owned land at Ophryneion
in the Troad and a farm at ⌐- - -⌐ on Thasos,[42] and the piece of
land on Thasos later mentioned [43] might also be his; (viii) one man
(unidentifiable) owned property at Abydos;[44] (ix) Alkibiades of Phegous
owned several pieces of land at Oropos;[45] (x) Charmides (Kritias' cousin?)
owned overseas possessions until he was deprived of them (Xen.Symp. iv 31:
APF 8792,IX); and (xi) Diodotos in 409 had an investment of 2000 dr. in
Chersonese, which was presumably in landed property since the interest on
it was paid in corn (Lys. xxxii 6 and 15; APF 3885).

---

(38) Hesperia 22 (1953) 249 Stele II, line 90. He was also working estates
at Mylaieis and Platauroi (ibid. lines 82 and 87), but their location
is unknown and may have been in Attika.

(39) Hesperia 22 (1953) 268 Stele VI, line 151.

(40) Hesperia 22 (1953) 249 Stele II, lines 177f. and 311f.

(41) Hesperia 22 (1953) 263 Stele IV, lines 17f.

(42) Hesperia 22 (1953) 268 Stele VI, lines 55f. and ibid. 287 Stele X, line 11.

(43) ibid. line 153.

(44) Hesperia 22 (1953) 279 Stele VII, line 78.

(45) Hesperia 22 (1953) 286 Stele VIII, lines 3f.

Though one of these eleven cases (Eutheros', no. (iii)) may (but
need not) concern a klerouch resident overseas, the other ten cases
should all be evidence for absentee landlordism, in at least one case
(Oionias', no. (v)) on an enormous scale. It cannot be reasonably
supposed that these were exceptional instances: on the contrary, it is
a fair assumption that property owning by Athenians abroad was a far
from trivial aspect of the economic unification of the Aegean during the
fifth century. Some Athenians at least did take private advantage of the
military shield provided by the Athenian navy to invest in real property
abroad. One corollary is perhaps worth adding. The fact that they did
so helps to give the Athenian upper class a cogent motive for supporting
actively imperialist policies during the fifth century and the Korinthian
War. The self-denying ordinance of Aristoteles' decree, which made this
motive inapplicable after 377, was domestically a major political blunder.

(4) The fourth source of wealth worth noting is risk capital lent out
at interest. Three particular facets of this are of importance.

(a) Bottomry loans.   At his death in 409 Diodotos had no less than 7 tal.
4000 dr. invested in bottomry loans (Lys. xxxii 6). This, the only fifth-
century evidence for the practice, is nevertheless enough to indicate that
merchant shipping in the Aegean in the late fifth century was being financed
in much the same way as is attested in detail from fourth-century speeches.
Some nineteen men are known to have engaged in naval financing of this kind.
It is simplest to tabulate the evidence.

(A) Athenian citizens

1. Diodotos (see above) (APF 3885)

2. Demosthenes (I) of Paiania; 7000 dr. on oan to Xouthos (Dem. xxvii 11)
   (APF 3597, XIII-XIV).

3. Archedemos of Anaphlystos: 1500 dr. to Apollodoros of Acharnai ([Dem.] 1 17), a loan made at Sestos for a trierarchy rather than a commercial voyage. We do not know how common this practice was, but few Athenians can have had international connections on the scale which Apollodoros had.

4. Demosthenes (II) of Paiania (Hyp. i (Dem.) 22: Plut. Comp. of Dem. and Cic. iii 6) (APF 3597, XX).

5. Demon (II) of Paiania; a loan to Protos (Dem. xxxii 15) (APF 3737).

6. Androkles of Sphettos; half of a loan of 3000 dr. to Artemon and Apollodoros of Phaselis (Dem. xxxv 10).

7. The speaker of Demosthenes xxxii, who may have been a citizen; a loan of 3000 dr. to Apatourios of Byzantion (Dem. xxxiii 6-7).

(B) Metics and foreigners

8. Parmenon of Byzantion; a loan of 1000 dr. to Apatourios (Dem. xxxiii 6).

9. Theodoros the Phoenician; a loan of 4500 dr. to Phormion (Dem. xxxiv 6).

10. Chrysippos the metic; a loan of 2000 dr. to Phormion (Dem. xxxiv 6).

11. Lampis the metic: a loan of 1000 dr. to Phormion (Dem. xxxiv 6).

12. Nausikrates of Karystos; half of a loan of 3000 dr. to Artemon and Apollodoros of Phaselis (Dem.xxxv 10).

13. Aratos of Halikarnassos; a loan of 1000 dr. to Apollodoros of Phaselis (Dem. xxxv 23).

14. Antipatros of Kition; a loan to Hyblesios (Dem. xxxv 32-3).

15. Nikippos; a loan of 800 dr. to Apollodoros of Acharnai at Sestos ([Dem.] 1 17; cf. no. 3 above).

16. Lykon of Herakleia; a loan of 4000 dr. to Megakleides and Thrasyllos of Eleusis (Dem. lii 20).

17, 18. The metics Dareios and Pamphilos; a joint loan of 3000 dr. to

    Dionysodoros and Parmeniskos (Dem. lvi 5-6).

19. The banker Phormion while a metic ([Dem.] xlix 31: Timosthenes of

    Aigilia, there mentioned, was presumably a naukleros, and Phormion's

    association with him probably consisted in putting up the money).

The preponderance of non-Athenians over Athenians in this list is
clear (12 against 6 or 7), but four of the Athenians have secured entry to
the Register. In spite of the risks of naval financing, the high rates of
interest which these speculations carried [46] offered a prudent man an
opportunity for profit which was obviously taken.

(b) Other interest-bearing loans. These, as short-term purely commercial
transactions, are to be sharply distinguished socially and economically
from interest-free eranos-loans (for which see Finley 1952, 85f). Since
they are to be considered here simply as a source of capital gains, the
distinction between secured and unsecured loans is not of prime importance
in this context. Money-lending at interest had been permitted by a law
which was certainly archaic in 384 if not genuinely Solonian (Lys. x 18),
and a catalogue of attested examples helps to reveal how widespread the
practice was. The plight of Strepsiades, owing 1200 dr. to Pasias and
300 dr. to Amynias at interest (at an unfortunately undisclosed rate)
(Ar. Clouds 18f., 739f., 1156 and 1285f.) typifies that attested in the
420's for Kallias (III) of Alopeke (Kratinos F 333, I 110K), Lamachos of
Oe and Megakles (V) of Alopeke;[47] in 409 Diodotos had 10,000 dr. lent

---

(46) In the fourth century they ranged from 20% to 33⅓% on an investment

    for a round trip from Athens to Athens: see Billeter 1898, 30-41.

(47) Ar.Ach. 614f. with schol. Lamachos was not initially poor, as

    Plutarch implies (Nik. xv 1 and Alk. xxi 9), his source being

    probably comic caricature; he had simply become so.

out 'at interest on landed security' ($\overset{,}{\epsilon}\gamma\gamma\epsilon\acute{\iota}\omega$ $\overset{,}{\epsilon}\pi\grave{\iota}$ $\tau\acute{o}\kappa\omega$),[48]
the rate of interest not being stated; the grandfather of a client of
Lysias lent Eraton 2 tal. at interest (apparently a fairly long-term
loan) at some indeterminable date before 404 (Lys. xvii 2-3); between
399 and 380 Aischines of Sphettos borrowed an unspecified sum from the
banker Sosinomos and from Aristogeiton at 36%, and paid it off by
borrowing from another client of Lysias at 18% (Lysias F1.1 Thalheim);
in 390 Demos was willing to borrow 1600 dr. from Aristophanes at 25%
(Lys. xix 25); in 376 Demosthenes the elder had about 1 tal. lent out
at 12% (Dem. xxvii 9); in 36 Arkesas of Pambotadai lent Apollodoros of
Acharnai 1600 dr. at 16% ([Dem.] liii 12-13); at his death ca. 360
Stratokles of Oion had about 4000 dr. lent out at 18% (Isaios xi 42); in
the 350's Timarchos of Sphettos allegedly bought office using money (3000 dr.)
which he had borrowed at 18% (Aisch. i 107); some time before 346/5
Pantainetos borrowed 4500 dr. from Nikoboulos and 6000 dr. from Euergos
in a complicated transaction whereby Nikoboulos and Euergos were the nominal
owners of the property which Pantainetos had bought with the money, and
Pantainetos paid them 12% which was nominally rent but actually interest
(Dem. xxxvii passim; see Finley 1952, 32f. for a clear summary); and
in 315/4 Nikogenes of Aixone, lent 420 dr. on the security of real property,
apparently at 7% interest. [49] Furthermore, Andokides' reference in 391
to overseas debts (And. iii 15) is illuminated both by the 2000 dr. investment made by Diodotos before 409 in Chersonese (Lys. xxxii 6 and 15), and by
the "talent from Peparethos" which Phormion assigned at his death in 370/69
as part of Archippe's dowry (Dem. xlv 28) and which was presumably an

---

(48) Lys. xxxii 15, with Naber's emendation, though see Fine 1951, 168f.

(49) Finley 1952, 127 no. 27; see ibid. 273 note 66. The dotal horos ibid.
156 no. 132, of 305/4, may also concern an interest payment, but the
exact nature of the transaction is still mysterious (see Finley 1952,
244 note 57, and Billeter 1898, 53f.).

interest-bearing investment.

These examples, deriving as they necessarily do almost exclusively from literary sources and therefore from the social class which could afford to pay for the services of speech-writers, probably represent merely the visible top of a practice widespread in all social classes: five or six of the 14 identifiable creditors in these examples merit entry in APF, and four out of the nine identifiable debtors. As with bottomry loans, the high interest rates which seem to have been normal partly had their origins in the normal risks of credit financing, but by the fourth century these risks had been at least alleviated by the development of techniques of debt-execution on predesignated property (see Finley 1952, passim), and comparison with the generally lower Roman rates - where the risks were no less suggests that Böckh (1886, I 158) was on the right lines in tracing the high rates in Athens mainly to a generally insufficient liquidity. The consequence - that the high rates offered a profitable field of speculation to a man, scrupulous or unscrupulous, who had liquid capital to spare - was to be seen in the generally hostile attitude towards money-lending in the literary sources, which not surprisingly reflect the views of the borrower rather than the lender.[50]

(c) Banking. Since, as has often been observed, Athenian bankers were fundamentally money-changers and money-lenders (not that modern bankers

---

(50) Hyperbolos' mother (Ar. Thesm. 842f.) is merely the first of an unending line of villains: cf. Dem. xxxvii 52; Dem. xlv 70; Antiphanes F 159 lines 1 -12, II 75K; Theoph. Char. vi 9; and the many references to ὀβολοστάται (LSJ[9] s.v.). Cf., however, Isok. vii 35 for an entertainingly rose-tinted view of the social virtues of money-lenders in making investment capital available.

are distinguishable save in respect of scale and stability), there is no basic functional difference between the kind of lending described in (a) and (b) above and that by which Athenian bankers earned their living. However, there are two important differences: (i) that the risk capital of Athenian bankers was not their own but their depositors' money (Dem. xxxvi 11), and (ii) that many if not most known bankers in fourth-century Athens were, or began their professional life as, non-Athenians. Consequently, they were dependent for their survival and social advance on their professional skill in choosing a good investment, and the need for a continuity of competence produced dynastic pressures within banking houses which are traced elsewhere (see APF 11672, I). Though there are two detectable cases where citizens appear to have gained substantial wealth by acting as bankers' agents (51)(and there were doubtless many more), it is on the whole fair to say that banking was not so much a way by which citizens became rich as a way by which slaves and metics were able to buy themselves citizenship. This was true, for example, for Pasion, later of Acharnai (APF 11672, IV and VIII); for Phormion, later possibly of Peiraieus (APF 11672, IX); perhaps for Aristolochos, later of Erchia (APF 1946); for Blepaios, later of Lamptra; [52] conceivably for Timodemos (APF 13674); and for Konon and Epigenes (Dein. i 43). This is not, of course,

---

(51) Pythodoros (I) of Acharnai (see APF 11672, IV and 12413) and Stephanos of Acharnai (see APF 11672, X). Antidoros of Phaleron may be another (see APF 1036) and so may Agyrrhios of Kollytos (see APF 8157, II).

(52) Cf. Dem. xxxvi 29; Alexis F 227, II 380 K; Dem. xl 52; Dem. xix 215; ii[2]1675, lines 29f.

to suggest that bankers were alone in using their gains for the direct
bribery of influential politicians (such as that of Demosthenes by Konon
and Epigenes) or for the more subtle and indirect bribery of ostentatious
generosity and voluntary liturgies; certainly analogous in purpose were
the choregiai of Lysias and Polemarchos (Lys. xii 20) or the donations
made in exploitation of the various emergencies of the years round 330
by Chairephilos the salt-fish seller (APF 15128), Chrysippos the bottomry
financier and his brother,[53] Eudemos of Plataia (ii^{2}351), Herakleides
of Salamis (ii^{2}360), Dionysios (ii^{2}363), Eucharistos (ii^{2}400), a man of
Miletos (ii^{2}407), Mnemon and [- -]ias of Herakleia (ii^{2}408), Potamon of
(?) Miletos (ii^{2}409), Philomelos (ii^{2}423), the metic Meidon of Samos
(ii^{2}1628, lines 366f : ii^{2}1629 lines 886f) and Pandios of Herakleia
(Hesperia 9 [1940] 332 no.39). Yet they were probably more rarely
analogous in effect. Of the men just named, Chairephilos alone is known
to have gained the citizenship, and his family immediately entered the
liturgical class. It rather looks as if it was mainly bankers, rather
than other metic entrepreneurs, who were able to amass a sufficient
investment in public goodwill to carry them across the social gulf that
separated them from the citizen body. It may be no accident that at
least three (Pasion, Phormion, and Aristolochos) and perhaps a fourth
(Timodemos) of the seven known enfranchis ed bankers are known to have
entered the liturgical class.

(5) The fifth and last source of wealth to be distinguished here consists
of political monies, bribes and booty. Since its essence is obviously the

---

(53)   Dem. xxxiv 38-40. Note the explicit admission that their
        generosity was 'in order that we might get a good reputation
        among you' (ἵνα παρ' ὑμῖν εὐδόξωμεν) (40).

redistribution of existing resources rather than the creation of new
ones, it stands apart from the four sources analysed above, and there
is the further difference that reliable (i.e. unprejudiced) quantified
information is almost impossible to come by. All that can be done is to
note briefly the politicians and soldiers who can be plausibly suspected,
or were so suspected at the time or later, to have owed their wealth, or
a substantial increment in it - and *imprimis* their membership of the
liturgical class - to bribes or booty. Of soldiers, three of the fourth-
century *condottieri* - Iphikrates, Chares, and Charidemos (see APF 7737;
15292, and 15380) - come into this category, though not, apparently,
Chabrias,[54] and the Korinthian War produced a crop of them: we can
point to Ergokles (APF 5052), Aristophanes and Nikophemos (APF 5951), and
Thrasyboulos of Steiria (APF 7310). It is hardly to be supposed that
their fifth-century predecessors were notably more abstemious in this
respect, but there is no certain positive evidence that one can quote.
Of politicians, the profitable political career of Themistokles (APF 6669)
was copied by many others from Kleon onwards.[55]   Already by the 420's,
as the Old Oligarch observed, much political business in Athens was being
transacted 'by money' (ἀπὸ χρημάτων   ; [Xen.] Ath.Pol. iii 3),
and the evidence does not allow us to suppose that the practice diminished
during the succeeding century. We know only one politician's financial
profits in any detail, Demosthenes' (APF 3597, XXI), but even so the
pattern is clear, ranging from barrister's fees and speech-writing through

(54) His father is now attested as trierarch (see APF 15086); there is
    of course the possibility that he was subsidized by his son, but
    the Platonic connections of Chabrias suggest a good social position.

(55) See APF 8674; and see below for Hagnon. For the fourth century
    cf. Aristophon, Kallistratos, and Demades, to name only three.

protection-money of the kind which Kriton paid to Archedemos (Xen.Mem.
ii 9, 4-8) to straight bribes, and was tolerated up to a point by public
opinion (see Brunt, CQ 75/11 (1961) 144, quoting Hyp. v (Dem.) 24-25).

There remain some minor sources such as tax-farming or activity as
a travelling merchant or retail-trader, but the number of men whose
presence in the liturgical class can be traced directly to one or other of
these activities is tiny: Andokides (IV) via naval trading after the crash
of 415 (see APF 828), and Chairephilos via salt-fish selling (see APF 15187)
are virtually the only examples. The lack of such evidence justifies the
tentative conclusion that on the whole it was difficult for such an entre-
preneur to secure large enough profit margins, or to operate on a large
enough scale, to give him major financial status. By and large it is true
to say that such new sources of income as were available outside agriculture
in fourth-century and late fifth-century Athens and were exploited on a
scale big enough to give the exploiter high economic standing fall into
one or other of the five categories analysed above.

In the chapters which follow it will be convenient, in analysing
certain facets of the social behaviour of the propertied class, to treat
the class en bloc irrespective of whether the economic background of its
individual members lay ultimately or immediately in agriculture, or in the
various new sources, or in any permutation of both kinds and categories.
Consequently, this is the most appropriate point to single out a major
change in the composition of the Athenian propertied class, since its
cause was, I think, the impact of these five new sources of wealth on the
upper reaches of Athenian society, and since there is a good case for
dating the period of its maximum impact in the last third of the fifth
century B.C. This change was the entry of nouveaux riches, sometimes of
allegedly dubious citizen status, into the propertied class and into

Radical politics in the years after 440. That the men who formed this movement were mainly industrial slave-owners is unmistakably clear, and it is equally clear that, with one notable exception (Nikias), the reaction to their advent as reflected in the contemporary literary sources ranged from (at best) irritated tolerance to bitter social resentment of a kind of which Aristotle's clinical analysis [56] remains by far the best description.

The first surviving indication that note was being taken of their advent comes from the 430's, when as the mise-en-scène of his Ploutoi Kratinos brought on a chorus of Plutuses who were to act as a jury and decide whether the fortunes of certain wealthy Athenians had been gained legitimately or not (GLP I 196 no.38): and even here Kratinos could discuss the fortunes and the civic statues of Hagnon of Steiria with malice, naturally, but without venom, and make him a 'man of long-established wealth' (ἀρχαιόπλουτος) on the strength of a sufficiently obvious pun. [57] A few years later, in his Seriphioi of 428-425, the tone hardened, and he was prepared to describe Athens as a 'city of slaves, of men new wealthy and wicked, dishonourables, Androkleses, and Dionysiosish barber-boils' (πόλιν δούλων, ἀνδρῶν νεοπλουτοπονήρων, αἰσχρῶν, Ἀνδροκλέων, Διονυσιοκουροπυρώνων). [58] It comes as no surprise that Aristophanes in 422 should compare the behaviour of Philokleon in his cups to 'new-wealthy raw wine' (νεοπλούτω τρυγί) [59], that so many public men of the period of the Peloponnesian

---

(56) Rhet. 1387a 8f. cf. Anon. Iambl. (DK⁵89[82]2, 8) for a pre-echo.

(57) Loc.cit. frag. (b), lines 32-33: " ἐ[ξ ἀ]ρχ[ῆς ἔχων] πάνθ' ὅς 'ἔςτ' αὐτῷ ".

(58) See foot of p. 70 following.

(59) Ar. Wasps 1309. Kock's Φρυγί is tempting, but τρυγί is paralleled by Ar. Ploutos 1086.

War should have been taunted as foreigners or slaves[60] in a way which
is much less common in the fourth century, that Thucydides' characterization of Kleon and Hyperbolos should have been expressed as it was
(Thuc. iii 36, 6 and vii 73, 3), that Xenophon should report the
exasperation of the experienced soldier Nikomachides at being passed over
for the generalship in favour of the merchant trader Antisthenes (Xen.
Mem. iii 4, 1f.), or that Phormisios' proposal, very soon after the
restoration of 403, to disenfranchise landless citizens, no matter how
rich they were, should have sought to express in political terms the
residual prejudices of the Therameneans (Lys. xxxiv 4 and hypothesis).
Again, there seems to have been much the same reaction in the late 390's
to the newly wealthy who owed their enrichment to the spoils of the
Korinthian War and Persian monies. The whole tenor of Lysias xix
represents an attempt to sidestep or divert popular prejudice and resentment against nouveaux riches such as Aristophanes and Nikophemos (cf.
Lys. xix 15-17 and 30) of a kind which a few years before Lysias had
deliberately exploited in his speech against Epikrates (Lys. xxvii 9f.,
quoted on p. II above).

---

(58) F 208, I 76K, with Meineke's necessary emendation Διονυς<ι>ο-,
 but the text remains uncertain and the translation is merely
 approximate. For the date see Geissler 1925, 31. Cf. also
 Eupolis F 197, I 312 K, 'I did not think that a city of slaves
 existed' (οὐκ ᾤμην εἶναι δούλων πόλιν),
 which, pace Hesych. s.v. δούλων πόλις, should be primarily a
 reference to Athens.

(60) Ar. Knights 44, etc., etc. A full list is quite impossible here.

I have the impression that during most of the fourth century
expressions of this kind were much less frequent than in the period
between 440 and 386. There is an occasional recrudescence, such as
Polykles' sneer at Apollodoros in 361 ([Dem.] 1 26) or, from the early
third century, Philippides' irritation at the ostentatious habits of
rich ex-slaves (F9, III 303K), but this amounts to comparatively little:
Harmodios' insulting reference in 371 to Iphikrates' parentage (Plut.
Mor. 187B) was remembered not for what Harmodios said but for Iphikrates'
devastating reply, and even the hostility to the new rich felt by the
speaker of [Demosthenes]xvii 23 shows how the social climate had changed,
for his resentment was not against arrivists of low origin, who had no
business to engage in a public career, but against men who had been
bribed by Macedon to act traitorously against Athenian interests. Indeed,
there is no better sign of the growing tolerance in Athenian society than
Theopompos' admisssion in that Demosthenes the elder of Paiania was a
'gentleman' (καλοκἀγαθός);(61) a hundred years before, such a
description for a slave-owning industrialist and money-lender like
Demosthenes, who owned no real property but a house and whose economic
behaviour - even by fourth-century standards - was more that of a metic
than that of a citizen, would have been socially impossible, an arrogant
paradox in bad taste.

It would be useless to pretend that a complete explanation of this
change is possible, but some of the relevant factors can be isolated. The
disappearance of many of the old landed families (see Chapter V), or at
least their disappearance as moulders of opinion, and the growing social
acceptability of some of the new families must have played some part, but

(61) FGH 115 F 325; cf. Aisch. iii 171 and APF 3597, VII.

concomitantly, and perhaps of more importance, there is a perceptible
narrowing of the differences in economic background. In the fourth
century to have a mixed holding, including both real property in land
and houses, industrial property in the form of revenue-earning slaves,
and liquid investments, became increasingly normal; Xenophon could make
Sokrates ask Theodote whether her income came from a farm, house-rents,
or slave craftsmen (Xen. Mem. iii 11,4), and Aischines could depict
Timarchos as a man who 'had nothing left, no house, no tenement-house,
no farmland, no slaves, no investments, in fact none of the means of
existence which decent people have' (Aisch. i 105). The mixed holdings of
Arizelos of Sphettos (Aisch. i 97-101); of Pasion of Acharnai (APF 11672,
V-VIII), of Kiron (APF 8443), or of Euktemon of Kephisia (APF 15164) can
fairly be called the norm for the fourth-century propertied class, and those
of Demosthenes the elder (APF 3597, XIII) or of Diodotos (APF 3885) a
divagation. Against such a background of growing homogeneity, it is not
surprising that nouveaux riches and new citizens seem to have been
accepted with much less social strain than in the fifth-century.

Chapter V

CONTINUITY AND STABILITY

That the liturgical class was not a caste is a truism. The
evidence set out in __APF__ helps to make clear both the fact that its
composition did change through the generations and the extent to which
this change falls into a detectable pattern. Such change has two
aspects, a family's biological continuity and the stability of its
economic position. It is possible to differentiate some six factors
which can be seen or presumed to have affected - in most cases adversely -
continuity and stability.

II   First, because obviously basic, is childlessness. Childless
marriages naturally occurred, and yet I know of no attested example
at Athens where childlessness was the admitted ground for divorce. Two
examples from Sparta are recorded,[1] and Plato (__Laws__ 784 B) envisaged
the ending of sterile marriages after ten years, but this does not amount
to much and certainly does not justify the a priori assumptions of Beauchet
(1897, I 379 with note 4) of a religious obligation to repudiate a sterile
woman. The reason for this silence is simple; Solon's inheritance law
permitted a man who had no legitimate sons to adopt whome he would as his
legal son and heir to his property.[2] By such adoptions, which were
clearly frequent[3] in the fourth century if not before, the effect of
childlessness could be very largely mitigated, and there would be a legal,

---

(1) Hdt. v. 39, 2 and vi 61, 2; both in royal houses, be it noted.

(2) Cf., for example, Isaios iii 68. See Gernet 1955, 121ff. and
     Harrison 1968, 82ff.

(3) Gernet 1955, 129 lists 27 instances from the fourth century from
     literary sources; and see Lewis 1955, 14.

nominal, and financial continuity even when there was none biologically. It is true, of course, that contested adoptions were common enough for the resultant law-suits to provide a living for lawyers such as Isaios, but this is not to be taken as evidence that adoption ceased to be a practical instrument for assuring continuity. The literary sources tend to be concentrated round the disputed cases, and adoption is one of the Athenian civil status procedures which until the Roman period is almost impossible to detect without literary evidence.

II   Nevertheless, there remain some cases where the failure of heirs is the most likely explanation for the apparent disappearance of a family from the propertied class. Though, again, it is almost impossible to prove a negative of this kine without literary evidence, this may well help to account for the disappearance of family lines after, e.g., Andokides (IV) of Kydathenaion, Perikles (II) of Cholargos, Leagros (II) of Kerameis, Nikias (III) of Kydantidai, and Timotheos (III) of Anaphlystos. The likelihood is that in these cases either there was no adopted heir or the heir-designate failed to make good his claim to have been adopted, so that the estate of the deceased passed to the members of his bilateral kindred (ἀγχιϲτεια according to rules which were capable of precise definition even if they contained an ambiguity and were sometimes flouted in practice.[4]   The fundamental point about these rules, in the present context, applies just as much to direct inheritance from father to son as to inheritance of any

---

(4) See Wyse 1904, 671 ff.; Lipsius 1905-1915, 578 ff.; [Harrison 1968, 143 ff.; Davies 1977-78, 108 with n.18]. The classic case of it being flouted in practice is provided by Isaios xi + [Dem.] xliii; see APF 2921. The possibility that an unclaimed inheritance escheated to the State can be discounted; see Wyse 1904, 576.

kind within the bilateral kindred: in the total absence of any law or convention of primogeniture the chances were high that a particular estate would not pass in toto to any one person but would be divided among a plurality of persons whose claims, in terms of genealogical closeness to the deceased, were equally good. The adverse effect of this law on the economic stability of families must have been very considerable. It is true that there is no explicitly attested case where the division of a property among new owners can be seen to have deprived them of the liturgical status held by the previous owner, but, e.g. the failure of the general Charidemos' three sons to appear in their own right in the navy lists of the 320's (APF 15380) strongly suggests that their father's position in the Three Hundred was beyond their individual resources. Similarly, the three sons of Mantias of Thorikos failed to inherit their father's position in the liturgical class (APF 9667); Thrasyllos noted, as if it were worthy of remark, that the brothers Eupolis (I), Mneson, and Thrasyllos (I) each inherited enough from their father to qualify for liturgical status (Isaios vii 5); the contrary was probably true for Stratokles and Theopompos, the sons of Charidemos of Oion (Isaios xi 40: APF 2921, XIV); and, at a lower economic level, the speaker of [Demosthenes] xlii and his brother, each inheriting 4500 dr. from their father, found themselves uncomfortably close to the border-line of the rentier class in a position which their father, with his 1 tal.3000 dr., had avoided by a fair margin ([Dem.] xlii 22).

This built-in tendency of Athenian estates to split apart at the death of an owner had certain perceptible consequences. In the first place, it helps to account for the high degree of geographical fragmentation in known Athenian property-holdings (see above, p. 52ᶠ.). In the second place, it accounts for the curious lack of emotional involvement among Athenians towards real property which they owned. One did not identify with

one's property in the way which is familiar in modern Western Europe:
rather, property was simply a machine for drawing an income from. Only
in terms of this comparative detachment is it possible to explain, for
example, how the implications of the antidosis-procedure - a physical
exchange of property - could be contemplated or followed through[5] with
equanimity, or how, when the Athenian countryside was evacuated in spring
431, the wrench which people felt was at leaving their way of life (δίαιτα),
their polis, and their cults, far more than at leaving their own personal
estates (Thuc. ii 16,2). Yet there are three aspects of social behaviour
which may be cited as symptoms that men sought to evade the consequences
of the inheritance law. (i) The first and most obvious is the exposure of
children and other means of family limitation, recommend by Hesiod for
explicitly economic reasons (WD 376f.) and clearly a common practice,
though its incidence in the propertied class is unquantifiable.[6]
(ii) Endogamy within the bilateral kindred substantially increased the
chances of retaining or re-uniting family property in one holding. In
the families included in the Register there are no fewer than 20 certain
or probable cases of such endogamy, and there are several attested
examples where the claimants to an estate gained, or hoped to gain, an
advantage thereby.   For example, Euboulides (II) claimed the estate of

---

(5) It is sometimes said that there is no evidence of an antidosis being
     carried through to the point of actual exchange. Lysias iv 1 is a
     clear case.

(6) The well-known statement of Polybios (xxxvi 17, 7) cannot safely be
     used as evidence for earlier periods, but cf. Men. Perik. 380f.,
     Poseidippos F 11, III 338 K, and the evidence quoted by Ferguson 1911,
     81f., J.J.B. Mulder, Quaestiones nonnullae ad Atheniensium matrimonia
     vitamque coniugalem pertinentes (diss. Utrecht, 1920) 130-134, and
     A. Cameron, CR 46 (1932) 105f.

(II) via his mother (aunt of Hagnias) rather than via his father
(Wyse (1904) 672: APF 2921), and Kallias' double route to the family of
Epilykos was the basis of his son Hipponikos' claim for the hand (and
estate) of Epilykos' daughter (APF 7826, XI-XII). It is safe to assume
that the improvement of inheritance-claims formed at least part of the
motivation for establishing duplicate lines of family relationship.

(iii) It was far from uncommon for property to remain undivided in the
joint ownership of the heirs (Biscardi 1956), in at least two known cases
even after the death of one of the original heirs.[7] Not only did such
an arrangement offer the obvious advantage of not splitting a viable unit,
but it may also have made dispersal more difficult and recovery by the
survivor(s) of the share of a deceased partner more straightforward.

Even so it is probably fair to say that these manoeuvres only
postponed the fragmentation imposed by the inheritance law. There
remained the possibility of exploiting the intricacies of the inheritance
law, the weaknesses or scruples of other people, and the abilities of
lawyers, by means of the systematic and ruthless acquisition of properties
whose owners stood or had stood within the bilateral kindred. This was
the method adopted by Diokles of Phlya (Isaios viii passim: APF 3443)
and Theopompos of Oion (Isaios xi passim: APF 2921), and was probably
the only effective available means of combatting fragmentation: that it
involved sharp practice, chicanery, and real injustice is probably another
direct consequence of Athens' failure to evolve a convention of primogeniture.

III The various forms of property available to Athenians varied sharply in
the degree to which they were or were not safe investments. That land was

---

(7) Lys. xxxii 5; Aisch. i 103: see Biscardi 1956, 108.

the safest of all is a cliché; Aristophanes and Nikophe os between 394
and 389 (Lys. xix 29 and 42: APF 5951), Timotheos (II) of Anaphlystos
between 394 and 373 ([Dem.] xlix 12: APF 13699), Nausikydes of Cholargos
in the 390's (Xen. Mem. ii 7,6: APF 844s), Pasion of Acharnai between ca.
386 and 370 (Dem. xxxvi 5: APF 11672, V), and the guardians of Nausimachos
(II) and Xenopeithes (II) in the 380's and 370's (Dem. xxxviii 7: APF 11263)
had all invested their ready money in landed property at the first
convenient moment. However, not all land was safe all of the time: the
property which Athenian nationals owned overseas in the later fifth century
(pp. 58 ff above) will all have been a complete write-off after 405, and
we know of several men who were ruined or at least adversely affected by
this, while by Aristoteles' decree the same will have happened to property
of this kind under Athenian ownership in 378/7 (Tod. GHI II 123, lines 25-31).
Again, in so far as the population of Athens was liable to drop in times of
stress, landed or real property normally leased out to tenants might cease
to be a source of revenue. Aristarchos was getting no rent from his
houses at the end of the Peloponnesian War for precisely this reason (Xen.
Mem. ii 7,2), and Athens was similarly 'deserted by its merchants and
foreigners and metics' during the Social War, according to Isokrates
(viii 21).

Other forms of property had their occupational hazards. With revenue-
earning slaves, for example, though the mass exodus of over 20,000 slaves
after or in 412 (Thuc. vii 24, 5, with Dover ad loc.) was due to entirely
exceptional circumstances and did not recur in our period, even the very
bad state of the evidence points to at least two important families, those
of Kallias and Nikias, as having been very badly hit thereby (APF 7826, VIII
and 10808): there must have been many more, particularly among the mine-
exploiters. More serious, because endemic, was the fact that slaves

depreciated as revenue-earning organisms, but there is no sign
whatever that the concept of depreciation was ever formulated. True,
we are told the terms of Nikias' contract leasing his 1000 mining slaves
to Sosias, which provided that Nikias was to receive 1 obol a day per
slave and that it was Sosias' responsibility to keep the number up to
1000 (Xen. Poroi iv 14), but that represents not an allowance for
depreciation so much as an unsubtle abdication of responsibility.
Xenophon's own proposals (if they are his) for the employment of publicly-
owned slaves in the mines include no reference to depreciation and replacement (Poroi iv 17-24). Since the problem of replacing dead or
enfeebled slaves would obviously arise in practice, the explanation is
probably that in small workshops the incidence of the problem would be
too irregular to be worth providing for in advance, while in big under-
takings it would be the responsibility of the slave or freedman overseer
(Sosias, Milyas, etc.) rather than of the owner. Equally serious must
have been the risk that the products of a particular workshop might fail
to sell. This was one of Aphobos' lines of defence against Demosthenes'
claim for the income of the dagger-makers (Dem. xxvii 19), and even if not
true it should have been plausible.

The remaining risks,those in thefield of bank-loans and interest-
bearing investments, hardly need specifying but should not be exaggerated.
We do hear of bankers going bankrupt (Dem. xxxiii 9 and xxxvi 50), but many
of these bankruptcies can be traced to the quite exceptional disruption of
commerical life caused by the Social War; again, though almost every kind
of money-lender's misadventure can be documented from surviving sources, it
should be remembered that on the whole the only transactions that we hear
of are those where something went wrong, and that to these risks as an
explanation of high interest rates should be added a probably insufficient

supply of liquid capital (p. 64 above).

IV   An Athenian politician occupied an exposed and vulnerable public
position. The most immediately effective way of undermining it,
universally resorted to in the fifth and fourth centuries,[8] was by
means of a political prosecution, since condemnation could damage or
nullify his political influence temporarily or permanently, while the
concomitant fine (if nothing worse) deprived him of civic rights until
it was paid and prejudiced his chances of purchasing his way back into
public life. In the present context what is relevant is not so much the
use of prosecutions as a weapon in the political dog-fight as its effect
on the chances that men whose ambition had pushed them into public life
would be able to retain their previous resources, let alone the profits of
their ambition, long enough to transmit them, in the form of a high
economic standing, to their families and descendants.

It is, I believe, fair to say that these chances were very far from
high. There were, indeed, front-rank politicians such as Xanthippos (I)

---

(8)   Cf. the list of fourth-century political prosecutions drawn up
by P. Cloché, Historia 9 (1960) 80f. Against Cloché's argument
that their number and importance should not be exaggerated, it should
be noted (i) that his list is far from complete, (ii) that there are
very few politicians whose career is known in satisfactory detail, and
(iii) that even if the comparative rarity of prosecution were a proven
fact, this would not diminish the importance of prosecution as a sanction or of conviction as a major personal disaster.

of Cholargos, Kleon (I) of Kydathenaion, Nikias (I) of Kydantidai, or Aristophon of Azenia, who are known or can be presumed to have transmitted such a standing to their descendants, in some cases, such as those of Miltiades (IV) of Lakiadai, Themistokles (I) of Phrearrhioi, Kallistratos of Aphidna, or Timotheos (II) of Anaphlystos, even after themselves suffering a serious condemnation. Yet there were many more for whom loss of credit, or the (actual or anticipated) adverse outcome of a political prosecution, or political murder, appears <u>on the available evidence</u> either to have been responsible for the end of the economic pretensions of the man concerned and his family, or to have been followed by a total lack of further information about him or about identifiable relatives. Into the first category come, for example, Pamphilos of Keiriadai, Agyrrhios of Kollytos, Aristophanes, Kallippos of Aixone, Aischines of Kothokidai, and possibly Autokles (I) of Euonymon: into the second come, for example, Paches, Androkles of Pitheis, Hyperbolos of Perithoidai, Kleophon of Acharnai, Perikles (II) of Cholargos, Theramenes of Steiria, the four ambassadors of 392/1 (Andokides (IV) of Kydathenaion, Epikrates of Kephisia, Kratinos of Sphettos, and Euboulides of Eleusis), Timarchos of Sphettos, Philokrates of Hagnous, and Phokion. It is perfectly true, of course, that much of the force of this argument is <u>ex silentio</u>. Yet this is not always the case,[9] and since in this particular context we are interested in a family's economic standing rather than in its sheer survival the composition of the propertied class is what forms the effective control, rather than the composition of the entire citizen body: and our knowledge of the composition of this class from the late fifth century onwards is respectable enough for the repeated

---

(9) E.g. the descendants of Pamphilos, known from Dem. xxxix and xl (<u>APF</u> <u>9667</u>), and the surviving relatives of Kleophon (Lys. xix 48).

failure of identifiable descendants of these men to appear subsequently
in it to be cumulatively important. As a tentative formulation, it is
fair to say that an Athenian politican would be distinctly lucky if he
managed both to occupy and to transmit to his heirs a position in the
Athenian propertied class.

V   A fifth potential cause of instability was the cost of liturgies and
the incidence of special taxation. Such figures as survive (principally
in Lysias xxi) for the costs of the various liturgies are set out in
APF pp. xxi-xxii. The figures cover a wide range, but it looks as if a
festival liturgy might normally cost from 1200 dr.to 3000 dr. and a sole
trierarchy between 4000 dr. and 6000 dr.   When compared with the minimum
liturgical census of 3-4 tal., these figures, representing more or less
regular and inescapable outlays of capital, are far from being inconsider-
able and could well have bespoken the major part of a man's income. To
them, furthermore, should be added the incidence of eisphora. Though
Ste Croix (1953, 49 and 69) has argued rightly that the 300+ tal. raised
in eisphora between 378/7 and Androtion's appointment ca. 357 as collector
of arrears (Dem. xxii 44) represented a levy of only 0.25% on taxable
capital per annum, it should be remembered that some quite large single
payments from rich men are recorded. We hear for example of payments of
3000 dr. and 4000 dr. by the speaker of Lysias xxi in the period 411-404
(Lys. xxi 3), of payments by two men in the late 390's totalling 4000 dr.
(Lys. xix 43), and of payments of 1800 dr. due from Demosthenes for the
10-year period of his minority (Dem. xxvii 37). Moreover,simply because
the levying of eisphora was irregular, rare, and unpredictable, the
individual payments might be quite large and in many cases would have to
be paid out of capital, or would involve the hypothecation of real property,
at the very moment when the fitting out of a fleet or the mobilization of

the army might well be making further calls on Athens' very limited
supply of liquid capital. (In the fifth century this would still be
true at the personal level, irrespective of the size of the League's or
Athene's reserve: even more so after 412). One may compare, for example,
the occasions on which Apollodoros of Acharnai was forced to seek loans of
one kind or another ([Dem.] liii 9 and 12-13; [Dem.] 1 13 and 17). If
Apollodoros, part-heir to one of the biggest estates in Athens and not
exactly a rustic, could find himself so short of ready money, it is
hardly to be supposed that the majority even of rich Athenians were better
situated.

Consequently, there is _prima facie_ a solid quantitative background to
the general statements about men being adversely affected or even more or
less genuinely ruined by liturgies and eisphorai, or to the individual
statements to this effect made by litigants about themselves or others.[10]
Yet this is not the whole story. Not only does it hardly need pointing out
that many of these statements or protests come from directly interested
parties, but also, unless the _antidosis_ and _diadikasia_ procedures worked
far more badly than the evidence entitles us to assume, it should have
been formally impossible for the liturgical and eisphora systems _by them-
selves_ as socio-economic mechanisms to push a man from a position of wealth
down even to a position in the _rentier_ class, let alone into real poverty.
The cause of the discrepancy will be traced in the next chapter: I think

---

(10) Xen. _Hell_. vi 2,1; id. _Oik_. ii 6; _id.Symp_. iv 30-32; Lys. vii 31-32,
     xix 9, 29 and 57-59, xxviii 3, xxix 4, and xxx 26; Isok. viii 128 and
     xii 145; Dem. xxiv 197-198, xxxviii 26, xlvii 54, and 1 8-9;
     Hypereides F 134; Ar. _Pol_. 1309a 15f.; Antiphanes F 204, II 98K;
     Dem. Phal. F 136 Wehrli = Plut. _Mor_. 349a; Diod. xiii 47, 7 and 52,
     5 and 64, 4; Anaximenes 2 (p.22, lines 5f. ed. Hammer). See Wyse 1904,
     396 and Ste Croix 1953, 69.

it will emerge reasonably clearly that insofar as there is a case for
supposing that liturgical and other public spending was responsible for
a loss in a man's capital resources, such a loss is to be traced not to
the place of such spending inthe economic structure but to its place in
the political structure.

VI   According both to Aristotle (NE 1123a 19f.) and to common sense,
inappropriate lavishness in spending is a moral. fault. It is pertinent
to conclude this list of the factors making against stability by making
what is perhaps an unecessarily obvious point,that imprudence, incompetence,
or a more general failure of character, on the part of the individual rich
man is by no means the least of these factors.   Kallias' susceptibility to
flatterers and parasites,[11] Sokrates' warning to Kritoboulos that unless
he gave his estate more careful management he would find himself in Queer
Street (Xen. Oik. ii 7 and 11), Timarchos' reckless living on capital
(Aisch. i 95ff), the conspicuous expenditure on artefacts by Alkibiades or
Meidias (APF 600, IX and Dem. xxi passim),or the large sums spent on het-
airai[12] form one half of the picture. The other, more nebulous but not
on that account to be underrated, is a simple decline in family ability.
There is a well-known passage in the Menon where Plato instances Themistokles'
son Kleophantos, Aristeides' son Lysimachos (II), Perikles' sons Paralos
and Xanthippos (II), and Thoukydides' sons Melesias (II) and Stephanos, as
men who in spite of an excellent education completely failed to inherit

---

(11) Eupolis' Kolakes and Autolykos, passim.

(12) Cf. Dem. xxxvi 8 and 45 (Apollodoros), [Dem.] lix passim
      (Phrynion, Lysias, and others), Ar. Ploutos 179 and 303 (Philonides),
      etc.

their fathers' arete (Plato, Menon 93B-94D). Aristotle put it more
crudely: 'A clever stock will degenerate towards the insane type of
character,like the descendants of Alkibiades or of the elder Dionysios;
a steady stock towards the fatuous and torpid type, like the descendants
of Kimon, Perikles, and Sokrates' (Rhet. 1390b 27ff). The trouble here
is that Plato elsewhere offers a slightly different diagnosis, in making
Lysimachos (II) complain that he and Melesias (II) had been allowed to do
what they liked (Τρυφᾶν) by preoccupied fathers (Laches 179 c-d),
and that in both contexts Plato has probably missed the substantive point,
that the skills which the sons in question had been taught - hor semanship
and wrestling - were inappropriate or irrelevant in the contemporary political context (see pp. 114 ff below). Yet even so, a failure of education
of this kind can be made good. The fact that on the whole it was not so made
good as to restore the sons' political effectiveness suggests that for the
families in question these diagnoses were on the right lines - and these
are merely the families in which surviving literary sources were interested.

Though for obvious reasons the effect of each of these six factors
taken separately cannot be computed, the evidence of APF does illuminate
grosso modo their general cumulative effect on the stability of families
inside the liturgical class. In what follows I use 'family' in a narrow
sense, to indicate the father-son-grandson inheritance-unit whose continuity and stability is in question here, rather than the extended family
of the bilateral kindred, and I exclude from consideration (a) those men
whose demotic is unknown (since the lack of a demotic makes the tracing of
a family line so much more difficult that the inclusion of these men will
distort the picture by increasing the number of singletons disproportion-
ally), and (b) those men whose only title to membership of the liturgical

class is inclusion in the Thousand (see Appendix I) or the Periandric
symmories (pp. 29 ff. above). My computations from APF yield the
following figures. There is one family members of which are attested in
the liturgical class for five generations; five families are attested
for four generations; 16 families are attested for three generations;
44 families are attested for two generations; and no fewer than 357 are
attested in a single generation only. These figures are startling, but
they are open to the objection that their force depends on silence and
ignorance. That this is not a decisive objection becomes clear if one
analyses the composition of the liturgical class in one particular
generation. For this purpose the two generations H (366-333) and (333-300)
offer the best control, since they are the best (or least badly) attested
and since we know enough about the composition of the liturgical class in
previous generations for the results not to be distorted to the point of
unusability by the loss of evidence. For this latter reason to carry
weight it is desirable to consider only those men whose patronymics are
known. Among them the 147 men in generation H represent[13] one family
which was in its fourth attested generation in the liturgical class, five
families which were in their third generation, 20 families which were in
their second generation, and 91 families which were in their first attested generation. In generation I the 164 men represent[14] among them one
family which was in its fifth attested generation in the liturgical class,
seven families which were in their third generation, 14 which were in their
second generation, but 60 which were in their first attested generation.

---

(13) The following figures exclude eight families which are represented in
     generation H in the liturgical class by both their first and their
     second liturgical generations.

(14) The following figures exclude one family which is represented in generation
     I in the liturgical class by both its first and its second liturgical
     generations.

Otherwise put, of 117 families represented in the liturgical class in generation H, the mid fourth century, 91, or just over three-quarters of the whole, cannot be shown not to have been first-generation liturgical families, while of the 82 families represented in the liturgical class in generation I, the late fourth century, 60, or just under three-quarters of the whole, cannot be shown not to have been first-generation liturgical families. The close comparability of the two proportions is superficially encouraging. It has to be said, however, that these figures may say something merely about the state of our evidence, and therefore say nothing of any statistical significance about the actual historical turnover in membership of the liturgical class. All the same, I think they have some suggestive value, and they are at least borne out by the only literary evidence on the subject, a statement by a member of generation I to the effect that 'to be continuously prosperous with one's property is not customary for the majority of the citizens' (τὸ διευτυχεῖν συνεχῶς τῇ οὐσίᾳ οὐ πολλοῖς τῶν πολιτῶν διαμένειν εἴθισται) ([Dem.] xlii 4). If the available evidence is any guide at all , what he says is the truth.

Chapter VI

PROPERTY-POWER

Even though the direct salaried employment of one citizen by
another may have been contrary to Athenian prejudices[1] and certainly
does not seem on the extant evidence to have constituted anything like a
determining economic pattern,[2] there were other, more indirect, techniques by which the possession of wealth on a large scale could be made
to carry influence in public life. The techniques can be seen to have
varied, and to have been variously effective, in different periods. What
follows is an attempt to describe these various techniques and to assess
their effects.

i

One facet of property power is perceptible particularly in the
fourth century. This operated negatively, as a kind of quasi-veto.
By undervaluing or concealing the ownership of property,[3] by dodging

---

(1) Xen. Mem. ii 8, 1-5 is usually quoted as evidence of this (e.g. by
     Jones 1957, 11), but this is in the mouth of an impoverished rentier
     whose distaste would naturally be sharper.

(2) Isaios v 39, Isok. xiv 48, and Dem. lvii 42 exemplify it, but this
     does not amount to much.

(3) Cf. ii² 1581, lines 1-2; Aristoph. Frogs 1065-6, Ekkl. 601-3; Pl. Rep.
     i 343 D; Lys. ii 24, xx 23; Isok. vii 35, xv 160; Isaios ii 47-49 (see
     APF 2921, XIV); Dem. xiv 25, xxvii 8 (see APF 3597, XIV); Dein. i 69-70.
     Not undervaluing as a sign of virtue: Isaios vii 39; Dem. xxviii 3.
     See de Ste Croix 1953, 33f.

liturgies,[4] by delaying the payment of eisphora or of naval debts until
the last possible moment[5], or by choosing not to contribute to a
voluntary subscription at a critical moment,[6] rich men could so minimize
the contribution of their property to the national revenue as to have a
serious adverse effect on the execution of public policy. It is no
accident that tactics of this kind are attested mainly in the fourth
century, while the testimony of Isokrates (vii 35; xv 159) that in the
fifth century men tended rather to overvalue their property is borne out
by the references in late fifth-century Comedy to men who laid claim to

---

(4) Lys. xxi 12, Isaios v 35-37; Dem. xxi 154f., xlii 22-23, xlv 66;
Aisch. i 101f.

(5) Cf. (a) Androtion's commission of ca. 356 charged with collecting
arrears of eisphora due from 378/7 to date (Dem. xxii 42-68, xxiv 161f.);
(b) the various measures adopted in 357/6 to secure the return of
naval equipment ([Dem.] xlvii 20f.); (c) the activity of the late
340's, reflected in ii²1622, in chasing up naval debts which had
been outstanding, in some cases for over thirty years (cf. lines
489-496); and (d) the swingeing punishment of ἁπλωϲιϲ τριήρουϲ
imposed on defaulting trierarchs in 326/5 (ii²1628, lines 339f.).

(6) Isaios v 37-38; Dem. xviii 312, xxi 161; Theoph. Char. xxii 3;
Plut. Phok. ix 1-2.

(7)

more wealth than they really possessed.   On the contrary, a very
credible motive for this change in behaviour lies to hand. The
presence until 412 of a large City or League reserve made it possible
to execute public decisions up to a point independently of the goodwill
of the propertied class, while the potential conflict of interest was
by-passed because the existence of overseas investments on a considerable scale gave the same class a vested interest in the effective execution
of such public decisions as secured the Athenian hold on the Empire.
After 404 neither of these conditions held good. In the absence of a
reserve the goodwill of this class was highly desirable, if not essential,
if the navy was to be effectively financed, and this change in the
internal balance of power at Athens coincided chronologically with the
new situation wherein, except for a short period in the late 390's (And.
iii 15), it was impracticable, politically impossible, or (after 378/7)
illegal, to yield this class its facilities for investing abroad and its
consequent fifth-century role as an interest group. All this is quite
enough to account both for the tactics described above, which were
evidently far from uncommon, and for the generalization of the 390's and
later that the rich were the peace-party (Hell. Ox. vi 3 Bart.; Ar. Ekkl.
197-198; Diod. xviii 10, 1-2).

---

(7)   Amynias (of Prasiai?: APF 12250) (Ar. Wasps 1268f. and Kratinos F 212,
      I 78 K: see G. Kaibel, Hermes 30 [1895] 441f.); Theogenes of
      Acharnai (Ar. Birds 822 with schol.: see A. Andrewes and D.M. Lewis,
      JHS 77 [1957] 178); Aischines (Ar. Birds 823 with schol.).

These tactics presuppose choice, and this is, I believe, the basic
fact about property as a basis for power and influence in Athenian
conditions: the possession of property enlarged the area of the
individual's choice in deciding on spheres of activity and course of
action. This appears to have been true for the agonistic liturgies, in
that within limits one could choose whether to perform one or not (p: 25
above). It was true for all liturgies, in that one could choose whether
to 'get by with the minimum' (ἀφοσιοῦσθαι   ; Isaios vii 38) or to do
more, even much more, than was legally necessary. Even more was this
true for financial acts of public relevance which were not in any
respect compulsory, for the performance of which wealth was a necessary
but not a sufficient condition - making epidoseis in money or in kind,
horse-breeding for competitive purposes, or the private financing of a
public building or utility. Epidoseis are well-attested from the 420's
onwards (8), and the theme of horse-breeding runs intermittently throughout our period (see pp. 97   ff. below). Privately financed public
utilities fall chronologically into two groups: (a) in the period 470's-
430's, Themistokles' telesterion at Phyla and temple of Artemis Aristoboule
at Melite in the 470's (see APF 6669, V), Kimon's public buildings and
works in the 460's (APF 8429, XVI), the Stoa of Peisianax ca. 460 (APF 9688,
VIII), the law-courts of Kallias (APF 7826, VII) and of Metiochos (APF 8429,
XIV) in the 450's, and the offer of Perikles' family to pay for the Spring-
house (APF 11811, VII); (b) in the 330's and 320's, the gates of Diochares
(APF 4048), Deinias' gift of land (APF 3163), the bridge of Xenokles

(8) E.g. Dem. xviii 112-114, xxi 160f, xlv 85, xlvi 13, lix 2; ii²1628,
     lines 339-452; Plut. Alk. x 1; Athen. iv 168 F; and cf. pp. 66 ff.
     above for the epidoseis made by metics.

(APF 11234), and Demosthenes' temple of Zeus Soter (APF 3597, XXI). It
is hardly surprising that there is reason to place all the donors concerned in the liturgical class, and noticeable that the chronological
pattern which emerges is similar to that attested for competitive horse-
breeding.

In their apolitical aspect generosity and display of such a kind
were so characteristic a form of behaviour as to call forth a specific
code of procedure for the propertied class based on the notion of
'munificence' (μεγαλοπρέπεια), fitting expenditure on a large
scale (APF xviii note 5).   In their political aspect they represented
a deliberate investment in the goodwill of public opinion within the
deme, tribe, or state. The interest on this investment was to be drawn
for the personal benefit of the investor; he was, or he fancied himself
to be, entitled to charis.   I think it is true to say that positive
property-power, i.e. all its exemplifications except the quasi-veto
described above, operates by means of charis, and that it is the variation
in the sphere of operation of charis which is the determining factor in
assessing the part which propert-power could play in public affairs. In
examining its workings it will be convenient to work outwards in scope and
backwards in time.

The form of charis most prevalent by the fourth century is forensic,
as a claim, on the grounds of civic, and particularly liturgical, virtue,
for favourable treatment from a jury if the individual investor came to
be involved in a law-suit. Examples of such a claim are so numerous and

unambiguous[9] as to leave no doubt of the way in which the investment
was expected to pay dividends. Five quotations suffice.

(i) Probably by ca. 420 Antiphon had formulated, as an exemplar for a
defendant, the argument 'Do not trust men who merit such punishment, but
you will see from my career that I am no schemer and have no acquisitive
designs. On the contrary, I pay many large war-levies, perform many
trierarchies, act munificently as choregos, lend money interest-free to
many and pay large debts as surety for many, owe my property to my exertions
and not to legal process, and am religious and law-abiding. You are not
to consider such a person as impious, or dishonourable' (Tetr.I β 12: for
the date Dover, CQ 44 (1950) 59).

(ii) In 402/1 a client of Isokrates said, 'Kallimachos is open to
accusation on many counts, his political style being what it is; for
myself, I will pass over all my other liturgies, but will remind you of
that liturgy of mine for which you would not only be right to owe me
charis (δικαίως ἔχοιτε χάριν) but which you may also take as
a pointer for the whole affair' (Isok. xviii 58). He then goes on to
describe his activities, as a trierarch with his brother after
Aigospotamoi, in privateering and running Lysandros' blockade, and draws

---

(9) Apart from the examples quoted in the text, cf. the reference to, or
    uses of, the motif in And. i 149; [And.] iv 42; Lysias iii 47, vi 46,
    vii 30-31, xix 56-57, xxi 12 and 25, xxx 26, P. Ryl. III 489, col. iii
    lines 60-76; Isok. vii 53 and xvi 35; Isaios iv 27-31, v 35-38,
    vi 60-61, vii 37-42; Dem. xx 151, xxi 153, xxv 76-78, xxxvi 40-42,
    xxxviii 25, xlvii 48. See Wyse 1904, 396. This is not to suggest
    that financial services were the only way of investing in charis:
    exceptional military service could evidently be equally effective
    (Lys. vi 46, xxx 26; Plut. Alk. vii 4 and x 3).

the moral: 'the person to whom you owe charis is not the person who has
suffered some private misfortune but the person who has conferred some
benefit on you' (Isok. xviii 62, cf. 67).

(iii) Soon after 400 a client of Lysias was brutally explicit: 'I have
been trierarch five times, fought in four see-battles, contributed to
many war-levies, and performed my other liturgies as amply as any
citizen. But my purpose in spending more than was enjoined upon me
by the city was to raise myself the higher in your opinion, so that if
any misfortune should befall me I might stand a better chance in court
(Lys. xxv 12-13).

(iv) Apprehensive in 349/8 of the effect which Meidias' liturgies would
have on a jury (Dem. xxi 98, 169, and 225), Demosthenes met it by counter-
bidding his own liturgies against Meidias' (a game which Demosthenes could
evidently play from a much better hand) (Dem. xxi 154-157) and by drawing
an even more pointed contrast: 'I am performing my choregia as a volunteer,
but Meidias' choregia was performed under the threat of an antidosis,
and one ought not to owe him any. charis for that' (Dem. xxi 156). One may
add the play made by Demosthenes with the sorry story of Meidias' voluntary
trierarchy (xxi 160-167).

(v) In 330 Lykourgos went a step further: 'some of Leokrates' advocates
..... will even cite their own liturgies in favour of the defendants.[9a]
These I particularly resent. Having performed them for the advancement of

---

(9a) Cf. the expected behaviour of Deinias on Leptines' behalf (Dem. xx 151),
or the actual or expected behaviour of Diotimos, Philippides,
Mnesarchides, and Neoptolemos on Meidias' behalf as πλούσιοι
καì τριήραρχοι (Dem. xxi 208f. and 216): partly a class closing
its ranks, partly indrect self-interest (Dem. xxi 213).

their own families, they are now asking you for a public token of
thanks (κοινὰς χάριτας   ). Horsebreeding, a munificient choregia,
and other expensive gestures, do not entitle a man to any such recognition
from you, since for these acts he alone is crowned, conferring no benefit
on others. To earn your charis he must, instead, have been distinguished
as a trierarch, or built walls to protect his city, or subscribed generously from his own property for the public safety. These are services
to the state: they affect the welfare of you all and prove the loyalty
of the donors, while the others are evidence of nothing but the wealth of
those who have spent the money (Lyk. Leokr. 139-140). Lykourgos' attempt
to circumscribe still further the area of influence of charis, by excluding
agonistic expenditure, echoes the contemporary disenchantment of Aristotle
and Demetrios with the agonistic liturgical system,[10] but was far from
new in 330. The lack of connexion between public munificence and
personal worthiness was always available as a motif of argument among
those who could not bid for goodwill adequately or at all in liturgical
terms,[11] while the illogicality of the whole argument from charis was
clear to Antiphon nearly a century previously (Tetr. I y 8). Even so,
the appeal to charis runs through the entire corpus of Athenian private
forensic oratory, and can fairly be supposed to have been a feature of
law-court speeches throughout the period, from the 450's to 321, in which
there was pleading before a mass jury. Its very persistence, in the face
of sound objections, suggests that it was not fundamentally a cliché
(though it may have become one), but rather that it incorporated an
important element of Athenian social thinking.

---

(10) Ar. Pol 1309^a 17 and F88-89 Rose; Demetrios F 136 Wehrli.

(11) Lys. xxvi 4; Dem. xxi 169 and 225, xxxvi 42.

Therein lies the point. The main value of the well-documented
forensic charis of the advanced democracy is not simply that it was
thought to influence fourth-century juries. Rather, it lies in the
fact that such charis represents an attenuated survival, and was a
translation into national and liturgical terms of a form of spending
for political motives which, older than liturgical spending and carried
on very largely at an international level, was of much wider scope and
importance than a simple claim for a jury's goodwill. In terms of this
older mechanism charis was nothing less than the primary basis both of
election to office and of preponderant political influence. There is a
survival of this in 388 or 387, when the speaker of Lysias xix defended
his father by saying, 'As to my father, since he has been treated as
guilty in these accusations, forgive me if I mention what he has spent on
the city and on his friends; I do this, not for mere vainglory, but to
bring in as evidence the fact that the same man cannot both spend a great
deal without compulsion and covet some of the public property at the
gravest risk. There are, indeed, persons who spend money in advance, not
with that sole object, but to obtain a return of twice the amount from
the appointments which you consider them to have earned. Now, not once
did my father seek office, but he has performed all the choregiai, has
been trierarch seven times, and has paid many large war-levies' (Lys. xix
56-57). Even as late as ca. 350 Meidias was apparently capable of quoting
his liturgies as a political argument in the Assembly (Dem. xxi 153) but
partly because there were so many others who could make the same sort of
claim, and partly for other reasons outlined below, such an argument was
less effective and therefore less common in the fourth century, surviving
mainly in the bribes offered by metics and in Apollodoros' frank admission
that his above average liturgical expenditure had at least partly the para-
political motive of ingratiating himself, as a new citizen of slave back-

ground, with the Athenian citizen body (Dem. xlv 78: APF 11672, XII).

The case is very different in the fifth century. Plutarch gives
an explicit formulation of the mechanism involved when he describes how
Nikias, unable to equal Perikles' aretē and eloquence or to compete with
Kleon's pandering to popular wishes, 'used his wealth as a political
base.... and tried to capture popular favour by choregiai and gymnasiarchies and other such lavish outlays (φιλοτιμίαι), capping all
his predecessors and contemporaries for expensiveness and appeal to charis'.[12]
Similarly, a generation before, Kimon's weapon against the pressure from
the Left in the 460's was his 'tyrant-scale property' (τυραννικὴ οὐσία),
deployed via munificent liturgies and poor relief to his fellow-demesmen
of Lakiadai of a kind startlingly similar to the Roman clientela (Ath. Pol.
xxvii 3). So too, a generation later, the speaker of Lysias xix wished the
jury to infer that Aristophanes' munificence in the late 390's adequately
accounted for the failure of Aristophanes' property to produce the expected
amount when it was confiscated (Lys. xix 29 and 42-44).

Even more explicit, and more valuable because contemporary, is the
opening section of the speech put by Thucydides into the mouth of
Alkibiades in the context of spring 415. 'Athenians, I have a better
right to command than others - I must begin with this as Nicias has
attacked me - and at the same time I believe myself to be worthy of it.
The things for which I am abused bring fame to my ancestors and to myself,
and to the country profit besides. The Hellenes, after expecting to see
our city ruined by the war, concluded it to be even greater than it really
is, by reason of the magnificence with which I represented it at the

---

(12) Plut. Nikias iii 1-2. I translate χάριτι as 'appeal to charis'
(LSJ & s.v., II 3) rather than as 'elegance' (thus Perrin), since
the latter, objective, sense is rare in prose.

Olympic Games of 416 , when I sent into the lists seven chariots,
a number never before entered by any private person, and won the first
prize, and was second and fourth, and took care to have everything else
in a style worthy of me victory. <u>Custom regards such displays as
honourable and they cannot be made without leaving behind them an
impression of power.</u> Again, any splendour that I may have exhibited at
home in providing choruses or otherwise, is naturally envied by my fellow
citizens, but in the eyes of foreigners has an air of strength as in the
other instance. And this is no useless folly, when a man at his own
private cost benefits not himself only, but his city: <u>nor is it unfair
that he who prides himself on his position should refuse to be on an
equality</u> with the rest' (Thuc. vi 16, 1-4 (tr. R. Crawley)).

The logic of 'expenditure' (δαπάνη   ) as a power-base is
nowhere stated more clearly than here. By that logic, a man who became
'illustrious' (λαμπρός   ) or 'visible' (φανερός   ) because he
was responsible for bringing glory to his city by the successful deployment of costly display in international competitions had a prescriptive
right to ask for a return from his city in the form of political or other
recognition. It is true, of course, that Alkibiades was speaking, and
Thucydides was writing, at a time when this prescriptive right was open
to challenge and to competition (see below), and this accounts for the
somewhat combative and defensive tone, but we are entitled to infer that
there had been a time when such a formulation would have been accepted
without serious question. It is, for example, the background of Herodotos'
remark that it was from Alkmeon (I) (i.e., in effect, from his enrichment
by "Kroisos" and his chariot victory of 592) that the Alkmeonidai became
'extremely illustrious' (κάρτα λαμπροί   ) (Hdt. vi 125, 1). It is
also the background of his interpolator in noting how it was from his
victories at Olympia and Delphi that Kallias (I) 'became visibly known to

all the Greeks by his enormous expenditures' (ἐφανερώθη ἐς τοὺς
Ἕλληνας πάντας δαπάνηςι μεγίςτηςι) ([Hdt.] vi 122, 1). It is,
furthermore, an extension of the emotional background of epinician
poetry, common to the international aristocracy whose exploits it
celebrated: 'in Pindar's system the Games provide a means by which a
man's worth is tried in action, and it is not until he has passed this
ordeal that he deserves praise and fame' (Bowra 1964, 178). Yet there
is this difference, that for Alkibiades, as for Alkmeon (I) and Kallias
(I), the point was not so much athletic prowess as magnificence and
display: the former might well carry with it personal honours (Bowra
1964, 184-9) and was attainable even by poorer men,[13] but only the latter
could provide the base of a really viable claim for political position.
Negatively, at any rate, what we know of the men in Athenian public life
confirms this: after Kylon and Phrynon in the later seventh century, the
only Athenian for whom athletic prowess is known to have been followed by
even secondary public prominence was Kallias son of Didymias (PA 7823), and
the kind of notice given to him, attempted or successful ostracism,[14] was
not exactly such as to encourage others to emulate him.

Not only in such a context was wealth necessary, it was necessary
on a very large scale. The only surviving figures - the 5 or 8 tal. which
Teisias of Kephale claimed from Alkibiades in compensation for the state

---

(13) Aglaos (?) of Athens may be a case in point: cf. Bacch. X (ix)
47f.

(14) [And.] iv 32; E. Vanderpool, Hesperia Suppl. VIII (1949) 409-410;
A.R. Hands, JHS 79 (1959) 78.

chariot of Argos in 416[15] - and the terminology of epinician and
other sources (see APF p. xxv note 7) all imply that what was needed
for 'illustriousness' (λαμπρότης) went far beyond the means even
of the average member of the narrow Athenian liturgical class. Correspon-
ingly, the group of families able and ready to undertake the expense was
far smaller. It is not likely to be a serious distortion of the facts when
we find that the 44 certain known entries by Athenians of four- and two-

---

(15) Isok. xvi 46 and Diod. xiii 74, 3; see APF 13479. This implies,
it is true, a cost per horse much more than the individual prices
recorded: though to pay only 300 dr. was being mean (Isaios v.43),
the two other recorded Athenian prices are both 1200 dr. (Ar.
Clouds 21-23; Lys. viii 10), which is likely to have been normal.
Still, the costs of selecting and of training adequately account
for the discrepancy. [The new evidence of price evaluations for
the horses of the Athenian cavalry in the fourth century (Braun 1970)
and in the third century (Kroll 1977) confirms this range of prices,
in particular by revealing that the maximum possible insurance
evaluation was 1200 dr. (Kroll 1977, 88f, and 99).]

horse chariots for international contexts[16] during the 300 years from
600 to 300 were made by the members of only fourteen families,[17] and
that three of these families (Alkmeonidai, Philaidai/Kimonids, and the
Kleinias-Alkibiades family) account for 25 of them.

The problem is to determine when and for how long this form of
spending was politically important. There are three ways of approach,
(i) by estimating the relative prevalence of 'expenditure' as a political
mechanism at various times, (ii)by **examining** the decline of the power base(s)
which preceded it, and (iii) by tracing the advent of the power base(s)
which supplanted it. Fortunately, a fairly consistent picture emerges.

The obly quantitative means available for estimating the prevalence
of 'expenditure' consists of the chronological distribution of the known
entries of four- and two-horse chariots. To an argument founded on such
evidence it may be objected that its base is too narrow to be other than
misleading, but the evidence contains no built-in distortion comparable to
that given to the trierarchy by the survival of the fourth-century navy-
lists, and in any case the argument does not stand alone.

---

(16) See Appendix III. These figures exclude the three dubious victories
   of Kallias (II) in the early fifth century (APF 7826, V) and the victories ascribed to Miltiades (II) and Kimon (IV) by [And.] iv 33, but
   include entries for festivals other than the four major ones. The
   prestige of victory in the former was admittedly less, but the cost
   of entry was not.

(17) This assumes that the father of the speaker of Lysias xix (APF 5951) is
   not to be identified with any entrant whose name is known and that the
   victor of ii^{2}3138 is not Demetrios. Otherwise the figure would fall
   to twelve.

Distributed by generation throughout the 300 years of the Register, the evidence divides as follows:

in generation A (600-566), $2^{(18)}$ known Athenian four-horse entries

    "   "   B (566-533), $7^{(19)}$ "   "   "   "   "

    "   "   C (533-500), $5^{(19)}$ "   "   "   "   "

    "   "   D (500-466), $5^{(19)}$ or $6^{(20)}$ "   "   "   "

    "   "   E (466-433), 5 or $6^{(20)}$ "   "   "   "

    "   ".   F (433-400), 12   known   "   "   "   "

    "   "   G (400-366), 1   "   "   "   "   entry

                and   2   "   "   two-horse entries

    "   "   H (366-333)   no   "   "   four-horse   "

                and   1   "   "   two-horse entry

    "   "   I (333-300), 3 or $4^{(21)}$ "   four-horse entries

                and   1 or $2^{(21)}$ "   two-horse   "

The striking fact about this distribution-pattern is the comparative failure of entries during generations G and H, in the very period moreover when the habits of the Athenian propertied class are known from speeches rather less inadequately than either before or after. I do not think that

---

(18) This includes the Pythian victory of Kallias (I), before 564, i.e. in 566 or 570.

(19) These figures include the six undated Alkmeonid victories previous to 486, distributed (admittedly arbitrarily) two per generation.

(20) Of the three victories of Lysis (I) and Demokrates (I), one should belong in each of generations D and E and the third is not assignable definitely.

(21) The contest won by Demades in 328(?) at Olympia may have been either.

this failure is an accident of our evidence; rather, it authorizes a
tentative inference that for much of the fourth century spending of this
sort did not have its former political importance; not because men
could not spend on this sort of scale (if Chabrias could, so could
Timotheos, Pasion, Onetor or Demosthenes) but because the men who could
so spend chose not to do so. Moreover, the beginning of such spending
can be approximately dated. It is probably no accident that generation
A saw a large increase in the number of opportunities for its deployment
and display. With the addition of the four-horse contest to the
Pythian Games of 582,[22] the foundations of the Isthmian Games in
580[23] and of the Nemean Games in 573,[24] and the reorganization of the

---

(22) Paus. x 7, 6: Schol. Pind. P. iii (II 62-63 Dr.); M.F. McGregor,
   TAPA 72 (1941) 279.

(23) Euseb. Chron. II 94-95 Schöne; K. Schneider, RE 9 (1916) 2249.

(24) Euseb. Chron. II 94-95 Schöne.

Panathenaia in or about 566,[25] the opportunities for competing for
prizes in organized contests and gaining international prestige thereby
had expanded in only twenty years from one every quadrennium to no fewer
than six. It is fair to suppose that this expansion was a **response to**
pressure, and that both the resources and the determination to engage in

---

(25) Pherekydes (<u>FGH</u> 3 F 2) and Hellanikos Λ(<u>FGH</u> 4 F 22) ap. Markell
    <u>Vit.Thuc</u>. 2-4; Euseb. <u>Chron</u>. II 94-95 Schone; T.J. Cadoux, <u>JHS</u>
    68 (1948) 104; J.A. Davison, <u>JHS</u> 78 (1958) 26f.; P.E. Corbett,
    <u>JHS</u> 80 (1960) 56f.; J.A. Davison, <u>JHS</u> 82 (1962) 141f. I am not quite
    so convinced as Corbett 58 and Davison (1962) 42 that the reference
    in <u>Marmor Parium</u> ep. 13 and (Eratosthenes)<u>Kataster</u>. 13 (quoted by
    Corbett 57 note 20) to Erichthonios as founder of the Panathenaia are
    'direct evidence for the belief that ordinary chariot races formed
    part of the proceedings from a very early date' or that 'it is surely
    hard to believe that if in reality they were first incorporated in
    the festival in the sixth century, their institution could be ascribed
    to mythical times' (Corbett 58). Wade-Gery's ingenious suggestion
    (1958, 154) that the conventional date of 1506 for the first foundation
    of the Panathenaia reflects something special in the celebration of
    506 deserves to be taken seriously, and we must never lose sight of
    the extent to which myths can be constructed, or traditions develop,
    in order to give a spurious air of immemorial antiquity to a new and
    perhaps contentious political creation. Most of the Theseus myth
    appears to be just that, and Stesichoros' <u>Oresteia</u> is a classic
    case.

chariot-racing as in other forms of athletic prowess had become available
in the first third of the sixth century as they had never been before.
Concordantly, we are explicitly told (Isok. xvi 25) that Alkmeon's four-
horse victory in 592 was the first such victory by an Athenian (though
it was not,of course, necessarily the first such entry). At least in
Athens, and probably not uniquely there but as part of a general movement,
the advent of this kind of property-power in politics can safely be
put in the first third of the sixth century.

iii

I see no alternative to the contention that what such expenditure,
in intention and probably in effect, supplanted as a political base was
cult-power, i.e. the control by genē of priesthoods and of institutions
which were centred on cults or defined in terms of them. Simply because
this form of power was under direct, sustained, and successful attack in
the sixth and fifth centuries, the positive indications of its survival
are few, but the chronicle both of the attack and of the survivals leaves
very little doubt what was in question. I conceive it to have functioned
in three main forms, which naturally slide into one another but are
worth distinguishing.

(a) The first is the control of membership of phratries.   Here the only
explicit evidence is the phratry-decree ii^{2}1237 of 396/5, whereof I can
curtail discussion by saying that I agree entirely with the analyses of
Wade-Gery (1958, 116ff), Andrewes 1961, and Thompson 1968 against that of
Wilamowitz (1893, II 259ff.). In the terms of this decree, the Demotionidai
are a genos, "an aristocratic corporation, with a position of privilege and
exegetic functions vis-a-vis the Phratry of the Dekeleieis" (Wade-Gery 1958,
127): in 396/5 the bye-laws of the Phratry were named after them, they
kept the Phratry's primary register, and they constituted a court of appeal

available (at considerable financial risk) to a man who considered
himself the victim of an unjust decision by the main body of the
Phratry to exclude him from it.[26] The point is two-fold: first,
these powers are to be taken as an attenuated relic of a time when
the Demotionidai decided by themselves, in the first and last instance,
whom to accept and whom to exclude; and second, until Kleisthenes'
reform the men who decided such things ipso facto decided a man's
citizenship status. At least five, and probably six other cases are
known where a genos seems to have been an organic part of a phratry in
much the same way that the Demotionidai were part of the Dekeleieis.
The known cases are: (a) Aisch. ii 147; the Eteoboutadai form part of
Aischines' phratry (see Andrewes 1961, 9); (b) Hesperia 7 (1938) 1 no. 1,
lines 76 and 79 ～ ii^{2}2345, lines 77 and 79; two men of the genos
Salaminioi are listed as members of the thiasos of Diogenes on a phratry-
register (see Andrewes 1961, 9-10); (c)(d) Et. Magn. 760, 31f.; the
Tikakidai and the Thyrgonidai were each both a genos and a phratry:
(e) Hesperia 10 (1941) 14 no.1, lines 17-18; the Medontidai are
attested as a phratry, but with an eponym whose ancestry went back to
Zeus in fifth-century genealogy (Hellanikos, FGH 323 a F23), it is hardly
possible that they are not a genos as well: (f) Isaios vii 13-17;
Thrasyllos claims that in adoption proceedings 'Apollodoros enrolled me
among the gennetai and the phrateres' (§ 13) at the altars during the
Thargelia (§ 15) without opposition from the gennetai and the phrateres' (§ 17),
i.e. that enrolment in the two groups took place at the same moment and by
the same ritual act (Andrewes 1961, 5 f.). Consequently, we are probably
entitled to generalize the information of ii^{2}1237 and to assume that in

(26) ii^{2}1237, lines 14, 20-21, and 29-44.

other Athenian phratries there was a similar development in a similar power-structure. Now, the Aristotelian tradition knew of a conservative revision of the citizen body (Διαψηφισμός) in 510 or 509 (Ath.Pol. xii 5), and traced a connection between Kleisthenes' admittance of neopolitai and that aspect of his reform which made residence in a deme the primary criterion of citizenship (Ath.Pol. xxi 2-4; Pol. 1275^b 34-37). The tradition has been questioned[27], I think, without good ground,[28] but even if in an extreme case both the diapsephismos and the group of men called neopolitai could be shown to be fictions, the conclusion would still stand, simply in terms of the content of Kleisthenes' reform, that there was an influential body of men in Attika in 508 who had a grievance against the then existing system of admissions to the citizen body and against the men who controlled the system. By setting up in the demes a route to citizenship alternative to the phratries, Kleisthenes inflcited what was, and was intended to be, the major defeat on cult power in its phratry aspect.

(b) The second aspect of cult-power which is worth distinguishing is the regional influence of local cults. Here again we are almost totally dependent, for evidence of its effect, on the measures taken by Kleisthenes in 508/7 to counter it, and we are too badly informed about the geographical distribution of the members of individual phratries in 508/7 to

---

(27) Wade-Gery 1958, 148f.; J.H. Oliver, Historia 9 (1960) 503f.

(28) The apparent identify of date between the diapsephismos " μετὰ τὴν τῶν τυράννων κατάλυειν"(Ath.Pol. xiii 5) and Kleisthenes' admission of new citizens " μετὰ τὴν τῶν τυράννων ἐκβολήν " (Ar.Pol. 1275 b 36) should not be allowed (as by Wade-Gery 1958, 148f.) to yield the inference that the two acts, of totally opposed political directions are identical. For Oliver's analysis see Lewis 1963, 37 note 135.

be able to determine whether local influence of this kind was partly or
mainly the same thing as the local cohesion of a phratry-unit.

The basic evidence is the case argued by Lewis 1963 that the geographical composition of the Kleisthenic trittyes shows signs of anomaly
or distortion, particularly in areas where there is reason to suppose the
existence of old and important local cult-centres or associations. Those
in question are the Marathonian Tetrapolis, Hekale, Halimous, the
Tetrakomoi, and possibly Pallene and Thorikos. Lewis's case is not
invalidated by the argument of Eliot (1962, 138) that the coastal trittyes
of Kekropis, Antiochis, and Erechtheis 'were so formed because they were
seen to be natural geographic entities'. This may well be true for these
trittyes (though see N.G.L. Hammond, CR 88/14 [1964] 187f.), but they
include none of the anomalies. In any case, even where trittys-boundaries
do appear to be geographically natural, the root question still remains
whether they coincided with the social boundaries of community and cult.
Moreover, in the light of post-1962 evidence we may now add to Lewis's
list the case of Erchia, taken away from its geographical neighbours
Paiania and Kytherros which together formed the inland trittys of
Pandionis, and linked instead with the Eastern and Southern slopes of
Pentelikon in the inland trittys of Aigeis. Here, the existence of the
'Greater Demarchy' of Erchia as a cult entity ca. 360-350 (Daux 1963:
Dow 1965; Dow 1968, 175) suggests that we have to do with a further
example. Paradoxically, the evidence can be strengthened by considering
two cases where, in terms of the neutralization of cults extra urbem,
there should have been anomalies in the Kleisthenic trittys-system but are
not; Phlya, the cult-centre of the genos Lykomidai, and Eleusis. In the
first case, the two branches of the genos were living at Phlya itself or
at Phrearrhioi in 508 (APF 6669 and 9238), and since there is no evidence

other Athenian phratries there was a similar development in a similar power-structure. Now, the Aristotelian tradition knew of a conservative revision of the citizen body ($\Delta\iota\alpha\psi\eta\varphi\iota\varsigma\mu\acute{o}\varsigma$) in 510 or 509 (Ath.Pol. xii 5), and traced a connection between Kleisthenes' admittance of neopolitai and that aspect of his reform which made residence in a deme the primary criterion of citizenship (Ath.Pol. xxi 2-4; Pol. 1275^{b} 34-37). The tradition has been questioned[27], I think, without good ground,[28] but even if in an extreme case both the diapsephismos and the group of men called neopolitai could be shown to be fictions, the conclusion would still stand, simply in terms of the content of Kleisthenes' reform, that there was an influential body of men in Attika in 508 who had a grievance against the then existing system of admissions to the citizen body and against the men who controlled the system. By setting up in the demes a route to citizenship alternative to the phratries, Kleisthenes inflcited what was, and was intended to be, the major defeat on cult power in its phratry aspect.

(b) The second aspect of cult-power which is worth distinguishing is the regional influence of local cults. Here again we are almost totally dependent, for evidence of its effect, on the measures taken by Kleisthenes in 508/7 to counter it, and we are too badly informed about the geographical distribution of the members of individual phratries in 508/7 to

---

(27) Wade-Gery 1958, 148f.; J.H. Oliver, Historia 9 (1960) 503f.

(28) The apparent identify of date between the diapsephismos " $\mu\epsilon\tau\grave{\alpha}$ $\tau\grave{\eta}\nu$ $\tau\tilde{\omega}\nu$ $\tau\upsilon\rho\acute{\alpha}\nu\nu\omega\nu$ $\kappa\alpha\tau\acute{\alpha}\lambda\upsilon\sigma\iota\nu$"(Ath.Pol. xiii 5) and Kleisthenes' admission of new citizens " $\mu\epsilon\tau\grave{\alpha}$ $\tau\grave{\eta}\nu$ $\tau\tilde{\omega}\nu$ $\tau\upsilon\rho\acute{\alpha}\nu\nu\omega\nu$ $\dot{\epsilon}\kappa\beta o\lambda\acute{\eta}\nu$ " (Ar.Pol. 1275 b 36) should not be allowed (as by Wade-Gery 1958, 148f.) to yield the inference that the two acts, of totally opposed political directions are identical. For Oliver's analysis see Lewis 1963, 37 note 135.

be able to determine whether local influence of this kind was partly or
mainly the same thing as the local cohesion of a phratry-unit.

The basic evidence is the case argued by Lewis 1963 that the geographical composition of the Kleisthenic trittyes shows signs of anomaly
or distortion, particularly in areas where there is reason to suppose the
existence of old and important local cult-centres or associations. Those
in question are the Marathonian Tetrapolis, Hekale, Halimous, the
Tetrakomoi, and possibly Pallene and Thorikos. Lewis's case is not
invalidated by the argument of Eliot (1962, 138) that the coastal trittyes
of Kekropis, Antiochis, and Erechtheis 'were so formed because they were
seen to be natural geographic entities'. This may well be true for these
trittyes (though see N.G.L. Hammond, CR 88/14 [1964] 187f.), but they
include none of the anomalies. In any case, even where trittys-boundaries
do appear to be geographically natural, the root question still remains
whether they coincided with the social boundaries of community and cult.
Moreover, in the light of post-1962 evidence we may now add to Lewis's
list the case of Erchia, taken away from its geographical neighbours
Paiania and Kytherros which together formed the inland trittys of
Pandionis, and linked instead with the Eastern and Southern slopes of
Pentelikon in the inland trittys of Aigeis. Here, the existence of the
'Greater Demarchy' of Erchia as a cult entity ca. 360-350 (Daux 1963:
Dow 1965; Dow 1968, 175) suggests that we have to do with a further
example. Paradoxically, the evidence can be strengthened by considering
two cases where, in terms of the neutralization of cults extra urbem,
there should have been anomalies in the Kleisthenic trittys-system but are
not; Phlya, the cult-centre of the genos Lykomidai, and Eleusis. In the
first case, the two branches of the genos were living at Phlya itself or
at Phrearrhioi in 508 (APF 6669 and 9238), and since there is no evidence

for supposing that adjacent demes looked to Phlya as their centre,
there was no point in distorting trittys-boundaries in the neighbour-
hood. Even more is this the case with Eleusis. Of the two *gene*
concerned with the cult, the Kerykes included families in Alopeke (APF
7826), Koile (ii^{2}1230: APF 10088), Acharnai and Hagnous,[29] and much
later Melite,[30] while the Eumolpidai included families in Paiania,[31]
Perithoidai (ii^{2}1934, lines 1 and 6), Eleusis,[32] and later Halai
Aixonides (ii^{2}3469), Peiraieus (ii^{2}2452, line 53), and Kydathenaion.[33]
Quite clearly, the important families of the *gene* were scattered throughout
Attika in 508. Like other *gene* such as the Brytidai which show a similar
scatter ([Dem.] lix 61), they were in no position to exercise a cohesive
local influence, and their power was not such that it could be effectively
circumscribed by means of simple gerrymandering.

(c) The third form of cult-power is that exercised through the more or
less national cults of widespread appeal and importance but under
gentilician control. Again, the evidence is largely indirect, consisting
of the means adopted at various times to neutralize or to circumscribe
such power. The chronologically primary method was also the more indirect,
the establishment of new festivals, which were not under gentilician control,
to serve as alternative focuses for religious expression to the gentilician

(29) See ii^{2}3510 and Kirchner's stemma *ad loc.*

(30) See ii^{2}3609 and Kirchner's stemma *ad loc.*: ii^{2}2342.

(31) Hesperia 26 (1957) 216 no. 66; Androtion, FGH 324 F 30.

(32) ii^{2}1235 line 13. Thrasyphon of Xypete (ibid. line 1) also belongs
      to one or other of the *gene*.

(33) ii^{2}2452, lines 48 and 59; ii^{2}3512.

cults. With varying degrees of probability the following cults and festivals can be put into this category; the Genesia, explicitly called a'festival at public cost' (demoteles) and possibly established by Solon, as Jacoby argued;[34] then the Panathenaia, refounded in (?) 566/5 and organized by hieropoioi;[35] the state cult, as distinct from the various gentile cults (Andrewes 1961, 7) of Apollo Patroos, the first temple to whom dates from the middle of the sixth century and may well, like the same Apollo's altar in his other aspect as Pythios,[36] be due to the tyrants; the Dionysia, **inaugurated in 502/1** [37] **to serve as the** cultic expression and complement of the Kleisthenic tribe-structure as it functioned from 501/0 onwards (Ath.Pol.xxii 2); and just possibly the cult of Aphrodite Pandemos, which had been founded by the 470's (DAA 318, no.296) perhaps much earlier,[38] and clearly of symbolic importance to Kallias (II) of Alopeke in 449 (DAA 152 no.136). The later, more direct, method was the much closer regulation by public enactment of already existing gentilician cults, i.e. their virtual nationalization. It has been persuasively argued(by Jeffery 1948, 109ff) that Solon may have begun

---

(34) Philochoros, FGH 328 F 168: Jacoby 1956, 243f.

(35) DAA 350f. nos. 326, 327, and 328: see note 25 above for the date.

(36) H.A. Thompson, Hesperia 6 (1937) 84ff: Thuc. vi 54, 6-7 etc. For the identity of Patroos with Pythios cf. Dem. xviii 141 and the presence of two omphaloi at the Patroon (Thompson 110f.).

(37) ii^{2}2318, as reconstructed by E. Capps, Hesperia 12 (1943) 1f.

(38) Apollodoros, FGH 244 F 113: Jacoby 1956, 254ff.

this process,[39] but the first certainly detectable example of it is
probably the Eleusis altar of 510-500 ($i^2$5: Jeffery 1948, 102) and the
two boustrophedon blocks from the Eleusinion in Athens (SEG XII 2-3)
containing detailed ritual regulations for the Eleusinian cult and
dated respectively ca. 510-500 and ca. 500-480 (Jeffery 1948, 102).
Then come the regulations for the Herakleian Games at Marathon shortly
after 490, including the appointment of a supervisory commission of 30
chosen in terms of the Kleisthenic tribes (SEG X 2 B: Lewis 1963, 31), and
the detailed regulations for the Hekatompedon, passed in 485/4 ($i^2$3-4).
A decade later the renewal by Kimon in 475 of the cult of Theseus must
have affected in some way the place of the local genos of Kimon's deme,
the Phytalidai, in the service of the cult.[40] The same will have been
true for the regulations made for the Eleusinian mysteries ca. 460, defining the privileges and obligations of the gene Kerykes and Eumolpidai
(Sokolowski 1962, 13,no.3), and for the redefinition in the 450's of the
'ancestral customs' of the genos Praxiergidai in the Kallynteria and
Plynteria (SEG XIV 3). Also part of this process were the various State
regulations for the cults of Poseidon at Sounion ca. 455/4 (SEG X 10), of
Eleu sis ca. 450/49 (the decree appointing epistatai)(SEG X 24), of
Athena Nike ca. 448,[41] of Apollo Delios in (?) 432/1 (SEG XXI 37),
of the Anakes ca. 430 (SEG X 59), of Apollo (Pythios?) ca. 430,[42]

---

(39) [I deal with this topic in more detail in a section on 'Late Archaic
religion and the state', forthcoming in CAH IV^2.]

(40) Plut. Theseus xii.1, xxxvi 1-2 and Kimon viii 5-7; Judeich,
Topographie[2] 74 and 352; Schlaifer 1940, 236ff.

(41) ML 44. For the mid sixth-century cult of Athena Nike cf. DAA 359 no.
329; G. Welter, Arch. Anz. (1939) 1f.

(42) $i^2$79, with Schlaifer 1940, 235ff. and Meritt 1962, 25ff. $i^2$78 may
concern the same cult.

of Hephaistos in 421/0 ($i^2$84), of Eleusis ca. 420 (the first-fruits
decree)(ML73), of Asklepios in 420/19 or later,[43] of Herakles at
Kynosarges by 415,[44] and of Bendis in (?) 413/2 (SEG X 64 = SEG XVII 5).
Comparable and relevant documents are also the sacrificial calendars
$i^2$840 and 842 (for which see Jeffery 1948, 109) and the calendar of
sacrifices for Paiania (Sokolowski 1962, 45 no.18). Practically the
last move of this kind was Nikomachos' omission of three talents' worth
of 'old' sacrifices from his recodification of the Athenian sacrificial
calendar between 403/2 and 400/399 (Lys. xxx 20): Dow's detailed argument
(Dow 1960, 286-291) that they were cut out of festivals accessible to,
and usually attended by, gennetai, allows it to join this same series.
Thenceforward, through the fourth century, there is much less evidence of
this type.[45] The battle had been won, and its results had been codified
by Nikomachos.

The picture here presented is of a sustained legislative onslaught on
the powers exercised by the members of genē in Athenian cults and Athenian
public life, beginning with Solon or soon after and going on down to the end
of the fifth century. Conversely, one may measure the strength of their
survival by a few direct indices: that the leader of the conservatives
in the 560's was probably also an Eteoboutad (APF 9251); that part of
Peisistratos' power-base as tyrnat was probably his influence over several

---

(43) $ii^2$4960, lines 9-13; Schlaifer 1940, 239ff.

(44) $i^2$129; Athen. vi 234 D-E.

(45) Regulations for the cult of Asklepios ($ii^2$47, lines 23f.) and for
Eleusis ($ii^2$140; $ii^2$204; Hesperia 26 [1957] 52 no. 9) exhaust the
evidence until Lykourgos, apart from three local sacrificial
calendars ($ii^2$1358 [Marathonian tetrapolis]: Hesperia 30 [1961] 293
no.1 [Teithras] : BCH 87 [1963] 603f. [Erchia]).

local cults (APF 11793, XII); that the Alkmeonidai, lacking any such
cultic connexions in Athens, went elsewhere for them, to Delphi and to
Ptoion (APF 9688,I); that Kleisthenes' competitors for prostasia after
510 could be sufficiently characterized by Herodotus mainly in terms of
their family cults (Hdt. v 61,2 and v 66,1); and that Themistokles' re-
building of the Lykomid telesterion at Phlya (Plut.Them. i 4) showed that
he considered his gentile affiliation to be a political asset worth
cultivating (and worth countering: Kimon's manoeuvres with Theseus (see
note (42) above) are probably a riposte). Yet in the 430's when the love-
lorn Hippothales wrote a poem about the kinship of his beloved Lysis with
Herakles, Ktesippos was prepared to call it roundly an old wives' tale
(Plato, Lysis 205 C-D). In 415, on a sensitive political issue wherein
they were directly concerned, the priests of the Eleusinian cult took no
active part in the process of deciding either to exile and curse Alkibiades
and others for a cultic offence or to recall him subsequently, but merely
acted as religious rubber-stamps for decisions taken by other men elsewhere
(Plut. Alk. xxii 5 and xxxiii 3).   Kallias' attempted (and unsuccessful)
invocation of his priestly status in 399 in his quarrel with Andokides
(And. i 115-116) is the last example of the deployment of a cultic sanction
in Athenian public life until Eurymedon the hierophant's prosecution of
Aristotle in 323;[46] and this, like Sophokles' law of 307 expelling the
philosophers,[47] has a very different background, that of the nationalist
reaction to international political theorizers with Macedonian support.

I conceive the role of 'expenditure' in the circumscription of cult

---

(46) Athen. xv 696a; D.L. v 5; Schafer III^{2}362 with note 2.

(47) Athen. xi 508 f. and xiii 610f.; D.L. v 38; Pollux ix 42.

power to have been this: it, and the massive accumulative of wealth of which it was a sign, was a means whereby a rich and ambitious family which was either (a) unable to employ the sanctions and prestige of cult power available to the members of a _genos_, or (b) considered them inadequate, could set itself up as an alternative focus for public attention to the leading cultic families and _genē_, and thereby indirectly appeal for a shift in political loyalties towards itself. Just because it was indirect, it had to be on a very big scale to make any impression, and even so it failed against the more direct deployment of wealth _via_ hired men or mercenaries which gave Peisistratos his power on two occasions.[48] Nevertheless, to place the Alkmeonidai and the Kimonids in group (a) and the Kallias-Hipponikos and the Kleinias-Alkibiades families in group (b) accounts for much of their economic behaviour during the sixth and fifth centuries, and gives what I believe to be the correct political explanation.

iv

The power-base which had very largely supplanted 'expenditure' by the end of the fifth century is now so increasingly well understood[49] that only a brief sketch of it is necessary. It has two aspects. In the first place, the fifth-century development of radical democratic sentiment and pressures placed a premium, first on the skills of the men who could give these pressures articulate expression as politicians and legislators, and secondly on the skills of men who could make a political

---

(48) Hdt. i 59, 5 and i 61, 3-4. Miltiades (IV) learnt the right lesson and applied it in Chersonese (Hdt. vi 39,2).

(49) Cf. Finley 1962, 3ff., particular 19ff.; Andrewes 1962, 83ff.; Kennedy 1963, 27ff.;[Connor 1971, with Davies 1975 and Lewis _CR_ 89/25 (1975) 87ff].

impression _via_ oratory in terms of the institutions - Council, Assembly, and law-courts - which embodied them. In the second place, the increasing scale and complexity of public and financial administration in the fifth century at home and abroad placed a premium on men who had the administrative skills and financial competence required to run the machine.

The direct indications of the date and scale of the rise of what may be called the democratic power-base are all familiar. They include, for example, the beginnings of self-consious oratorical theory and training in the work of the Sicilian rhetoricians and of the Sophists (Kennedy 1963, 26ff. and 52ff); the shift from the private patronage of public works such as those of the 460's (p. 91 above) to the predominance of projects initiated and financed by or through the City; the rigorously detailed published accounting required, from the 450's onwards, of the various administrative boards;[50] the prominent position given in fifth-

---

(50) E.g. of the Hellenotamiai from 454 onwards, of the tamiai of Athens for borrowings from the time of the Samian revolt onwards, of the tamiai of Athens for the Parthenon treasures from 434 onwards and of the tamiai of the other gods from the same date, and of the various building commissions down to the extraordinary (and, one might have thought, unnecessary) detail of the Erechtheion building accounts from 409 onwards.

century documents to the secretary of the Council, amounting to little
less than his elevation to the status of eponymous magistrate, and the
calibre of some of the men known to have held the office;[51] the pains
which many public men took to identify themselves with the interests and
values of the common people (Connor 1971); and the extent to which both
persuasiveness and financial activity become salient characteristics
of the political activity of public men.

Moreover, the indirect indications, though more difficult to evaluate,
make it quite clear that the political class changed not only in behaviour
but also in composition.

(1) The advent of men in the political class in the second half of the
fifth century, whose background lay in industrial slave-owning of one
kind or another, was traced in chapter IV. Almost without exception they
are men of the Radical Left. For only one of them are we told, or there
is any good reason to suppose, that the financial resources provided by
such a background were deployed in ways comparable to the older politically-

---

(51) Identifications and evaluation are unpleasantly hazardous, but cf.,
from the propertied class, Hipponikos of Alopeke ($i^2$359, line 5:
new reading by D.M. Lewis), Polyaratos of Cholargos ($i^2$125, line 5),
Kephisophon of Paiania ($ii^2$1, line 1), and Stephanos of Alopeke
(Athen. vi 234E), and among politicians and generals, Pasiphon of
Phrearrhioi (SEG X 64), Agyrrhios ($ii^2$2), Pleistias ($i^2$63, lines 56
and 59: PA 11864), Neokleides (Wade-Gery 1958, 208f.: = PA 10631),
Phantokles ($i^2$75, line 1: = PA 14114), Charoiades ($i^2$56, line 11: =
PA 15529?), and possibly Archestratos ($i^2$358 = AFD 36f., line 5:
= PA 2411?).

intended 'expenditure'. It is hardly chance that this one[52] man, the
general Nikias of Kydantidai (Plut. Nikias iii 1-2), was also the only
man with this background whom later historians characterized as a gentleman and as leader of the 'notables' (ἐπιφανεῖς) (Ath.Pol. xxviii 3
and 5). For the other men with this background, their wealth was politically
valuable merely insofar as it gave them the income and leisure to pursue
full-time political activity, and in no other way.

The contrast became even sharper when men from unequivocally poor
backgrounds began to make their way into civilian public life, able to
re ly on oratorical and forensic ability alone even without formal
rhetorical training. Demades is perhaps the most notable example of
this group[53], but he was far from being unique or the earliest:
Archedemos of Pelekes was probably comparable (Xen.Mem. ii 9,4-8), as
were Epikrates (Lys. xxvii 9-10), Stephanos ([Dem.] lix 42), and possibly
Aristogeiton ([Dem.] xxv 65) and doubtless others from the sycophantic
fringe of political life of whom we know nothing.
(2) Given that in Athens marriages were a matter of contractual
arrangement between the father or master (κύριοc) of the woman
and her husband, each side seeking the most advantageous arrangement in
terms of property and social position, it is only to be expected that
when such marriages occurred in political circles they might be the
result of a calculation in terms of political advantage as well, and
might symbolize an alliance or a rapprochement in the style, e.g. of
Pompeius' marriage to Julia, and thereby also serve as a manifesto to
public opinion. To identify and typify all the perceptible marriages

---

(52) Teisias of Kephale, friend of Alkibiades, might conceivably be a
    second, but we know nothing of his economic background (see APF
    13479). He is best left sub judice.

(53) Demad. F 55 de Falco; Suda Δ 414-415 etc. see APF 3263.

of this kind is far from easy, partly because there is no clear line of
demarcation between those marriages which are political and those which
are not, and partly because the import of a marriage cannot well be
calculated unless something is known of the father of the woman concerned,
and the available evidence tends to be even poorer here than for patri-
lineal descent. For example, men such as Charias the father-in-law of
Leogoras (I) (And. i 106) or Kallias the father-in-law of Hippias the
tyrant (Thuc. vi 55, 1) are nonentities to us, but unlikely to have
been so in fact, while in our ignorance even of their fathers' names a
proper appreciation of the importance of the woman who married first
Stesagoras and then Kypselos (APF 8429,V), or of the woman who married
first Perikles and then Hipponikos (II)(APF 7826,IX), cannot even begin.

Nevertheless, marriages which from what is known of the contracting
parties may fairly be regarded as political were so common and persistent
an element in Athenian public life that they provide no small part of the
evidence for analysing Athenian politics in primarily dynastic terms.
Virtually the first acts by named historical Athenians of which we know
anything - Kylon's marriage to the daughter of Theagenes of Megara,
probably in the 630's (Thuc. i 126,3; Pausx. i 28,1) and Agamestor's
marriage to the daughter of Kypselos of Korinth ca. 630 (APF 8429,II) -
exemplify one type of political marriage, the link with a ruling house
outside Athens. Such marriages continued through the sixth century,
as shown by the marriage of Megakles (II) to Agariste (I) of Sikyon
(Hdt. vi 126f.,), the marriage of Peisistratos to Timonassa, the former
wife of Archinos of Ambrakia (Hdt. v 94, 1; Ath.Pol. xvii 4), and the
marriage of Hippias' daughter Archedike to Aiantides of Lampsakos (Thuc.
vi 59,3). They seem to have lapsed during the fifth century, even before
Perikles' citizenship law of 451/0, but reappeared in the fourth century
with the links contracted by the condottieri with the Thracian princes

(APF Table VI) and the marriages of the Kimonid Euthydike to
Ophelas of Kyrene and subsequently to Demetrios Poliorketes (Diod. xx 40,5;
Plut.Demetr. xiv 1-2).

More widespread, naturally, are internal links within Athenian
society. Into this category come, for instance, the marriages contracted
by the Peisistratidai, with the daughters of Megakles (II) and Charmos
of Kollytos (APF 11793, VI-VII), or the great dynastic coalescence of the
480's between the Alkmeonids, Kimonids, and Kerykes, represented by the
marriages of Kimon (II) to Isodike, of Kimon's sister to Thoukydides (I),
and of Kallias (II) to Elpinike (see APF 8429, XII and Table I). Similarly,
from the 450's to the 420's the families of Perikles, Teisandros, Kallias,
Kleinias, Glaukon, and Andokides conglobulated themselves into a virtual
Whig aristocracy with the marriages of Xanthippos (II), Glaukon (II), and
Leogoras (II) to daughters of Teisandros (II), of Hipponikos (II) to
Perikles' ex-wife, of Kallias (III) to the daughter of Glaukon (II), and
of Alkibiades (III) to Hipparete (I) (See APF Table 1). Closely analogous
was the creation, in the second and third generations of the fifth century,
of a Radical aristocracy formed by the Gephyraioi and the families of
Kleon, Dikaiogenes, Thoudippos, and Polyaratos via the marriages of
Harmodios (II) and Kleon (I) to daughters of Dikaiogenes (I), of Polyaratos
(I) and Kephisophon (I) to daughters of Menexenos (I), of Thoudippos (I) to
Kleon's daughter, of Mantias, Kleomedon (I), and Chabrias' brother-in-law
Eryximachos (II) to daughters of Polyaratos (I), and of Mantias to Pamphilos'
daughter (See APF Table II). Also similar were the early fourth-century
links between Thrasyboulos and Nikias (II) ca. 390 (Dem. xix 290: APF
10808) or between Agyrrhios, Kallistratos, and Timomachos (APF 8157).

What is extraordinarily difficult is to carry this series of internal
political marriages further down through the fourth century. The last two
marriages which can reasonably be supposed to have carried, or to have

been intended to carry, any politically programmatic value at the time
they were contracted are Timomachos' marriage to the daughter of
Kallistratos ca. 370 (APF 8157) and Diophantos' marriage to the daughter
of Melanopos (II) of Aixone at about the same date.[54] Thereafter,
throughout what is by Athenian standards an exceptionally well-documented
period of over 40 years until the regime of Demetrios, there is not a
single certain discernible marriage-link between any two men within the
circle of the major or the minor civilian politicians. The only apparent
exception to this statement is the marriage of Iphikrates' son Menestheus
to the daughter of Timotheos in 362 ([Dem.] xlix 66: see APF 7737), but
it is not a real exception for the very reason that all those concerned
were military men first and foremost and owed their public position to
that fact. That this lack of evidence for marriage-links should be due
to accident is hardly credible.   Rather the conclusion should be that
the contraction of marriage had ceased to play any effective part in
political manoeuvring, and that the post-370 generation of politicians
realized this and acted accordingly, relying instead on their professional
skills as orators and administrators to carry them towards a position of
political pre-eminence.

(3) To a greater or lesser extent most of the major political figures of
the sixth century and of the first two-thirds of the fifth century either
initiated a political tradition, to be continued by their sons and grand-
sons, or were themselves heirs to such a tradition. Again, there are two
obvious exceptions (on our present evidence), Themistokles and Ephialtes,

(54) I think this is the most likely form of the link which made
     Diophantos the κηδεςτής of Melanopos (Harp. s.v. Μελάνωπος)
     and gave Diophantos a son, also named Melanopos and adult in the 340's
     ([Dem.] xxxv 6). I hope to discuss Melanopos' family elsewhere.

and they are two of the men principally responsible for a political

climate wherein after the 430's the value of a political inheritance of

this kind apparently diminished very considerably among non-military

public figures. There are admittedly not a few civilian politicians

of the fourth century whose fathers are known to have been politically

active, including some major figures - Androtion son of Andron, Periandros

son of Polyaratos, Habron son of Lykourgos, and possibly Aristonikos son

of Aristoteles[55] - as well as a scatter of more minor figures such as

Demostratos son of Aristophon, Thrasyboulos son of Thrasyboulos of

Steiria, Polyeuktos son of Timokrates, and Demeas son of Demades. In

itself, this phenomenon is is not in the least surprising: in a small

community, and with an even smaller class able to participate directly

in political life in the absence of adequate assured and legitimate

remuneration, it would be in the highest degree remarkable if this did

not happen. Yet, in contrast to, e.g. the six or more continuous gen-

erations of political activity attested for the Alkmeonidai, at least

five for the Kimonids and the families of Andokides and Kallias, and at

least three for the families of Perikles and Alkibiades, in only two

families active between 400 and 300 B.C. is a comparable continuous family

political tradition from father to son known to have extended beyond the

second generation; and one of them, the Strombichos-Diotimos family of

Euonymon, was first and foremost a military family, not a civilian one.

(The other is the succession Demades (I) - Demeas (II) - Demades (II).)

Unless our evidence is seriously misleading, it looks as if in fourth-

century conditions the impetus generated by the civilian political career

---

(55) For this last filiation see Lewis 1959, 239-241.

of one man, however successful, tended to be insufficient to carry a
family position in the political class beyond his son.

v

To this picture the field of public activity represented by the
higher military offices presents a sharp contrast. Not only did the men
who filled the offices tend to be in the propertied class, but even
under the full democracy they also tended to come from, or to found,
military dynasties of the type exemplified by the Barkids and Magonids
at Carthage. The evidence for this statement is set out in Appendix II,
and can be summarized as follows. Of 20 identifiable taxiarchs, two
qualify directly, and another one indirectly, for inclusion in APF. Of
27 identifiable phylarchs, none qualify directly, and five indirectly,
for, inclusion. Of 31 identifiable hipparchs, six qualify directly, and
four indirectly, for inclusion. Of 252 identifiable generals, 47 qualify
directly, and 43 indirectly, for inclusion. That is to say, the overlap
between the propertied class and the military office holders rises
steadily through the military cursus,[56] so that over one-third of known
hipparchs and generals qualify directly or indirectly for APF. However,

---

(56) For the existence of the cursus cf. Ar. Birds 799; Xen.Mem. iii 4,1;
   and Theophrastos, Frag.Vat. de eligendis magistratibus (ed.W.Aly, Studi
   e Testi 104, Vatican City, 1943) Fol.B. 172-183. It could clearly be
   short circuited, as by Kleon and Antisthenes (though they were both
   knights, interestingly enough: schol. Ar.Knights 225 and Xen. Mem.
   iii 4, 1), but can be presumed to have been the normal practice.

even so this underestimates the extent of the overlap, because these figures include men whose demotic is unknown. If this distinction is recognized, the figures are even more remarkable, viz:-

Taxiarchs:	demotics known 11;	of these	1 qualifies for	APF
	" unknown 9;	" "	2	"	"	"
Phylarchs:	" known 17;	" "	4	"	"	"
	" unknown 10;	" "	1	"	"	"
Hipparchs:	" known 23;	" "	9	"	"	"
	" unknown 8;	" "	1	"	"	"
Generals:	" known 131;	" "	80	"	"	"
	" unknown 122;	" "	7	"	"	"

Among men with known demotic, again, the overlap within the propertied class rises steadily through the military hierarchy, reaching 39% for the hipparchs and 61% for the generals. That the corresponding proportions for men of unknown demotic are so low indicates with disconcerting force how dependent we are on the survival of demotics for compiling demographic information of any value whatever. In the light of these figures the remarks of the Old Oligarch ([Xen.] Ath.Pol. i 3) and Aristotle (Pol. 1282^a 31-32) to the effect that the recruiting field for the military offices was 'those of good family' (χρηστοί) or the 'well-off' (εὐποροι) can be given quantitative confirmation: this was, and in spite of Theophrastos' doubts as to the wisdom of the practice[57] continued to be, no

---

(57) Frag.Vat. (note 56) Fol.B., 8-88. Theophrastos' four Athenian examples of generals who would not have gained office under timokratic rules - Iphikrates, Chabrias, Aristeides, Themistokles - were ill-chosen; for only one of them, Iphikrates, is there any good reason to suppose that he came from a family outside the rentier class. Charidemos and Chares would have been nearer the mark.

124

less than the truth.

The complement to this practice was the development of 'family houses which have held the generalship' (οἶκοι ἐϲτρατηγηκότεϲ). Their existence was deduced long ago from literary evidence[58] and some of them were traced by Sundwall (1906, 30): they can now be seen to have been so widespread as to be little less than the prevailing custom. Some 23 such 'houses' can be detected with reasonable certainty, and another three with varying degrees of probability, to have each provided at least two military officials (see Appendix II, left column, for these attributions). 58 of the known generals come from these 'houses' (excluding doubtful cases), and 18 out of the 26 'houses' represent families which have merited inclusion in APF. Given the endemic difficulties of safe identification and our painfully imperfect knowledge both of the propertied class, for much of our period, and of the less distinguished military officials throughout the period, such figures allow the presumption that the military offices were to a considerable extent filled by what was de facto a hereditary caste, and that though recruitment to it might well be made in the first instance on the basis of merit from poor men, the correlation between the caste and the propertied class always remained high.

This contrast between a largely dynastic military caste, closely tied to property, and a much more fluid and open, largely non-dynastic, political class is an undoubted fact. That there was a contrast, and that the two occupations - of general and of politician - had become very largely separate by the fourth century was seen by contemporaries and

(58) Hauvette-Besnault 48-49: cf. And. i 146; Xen. Hell. vi 3, 4; Dem. xxxiv 50; Aisch. i 27.

reflected in their terminology. For Lysias, in a context of 405/4, the categories 'political leaders' and 'generals and taxiarchs' were capable of being distinguished (Lys. xiii 7f.; see Lewis, 1961, 123. Cf. Dem. ix 38 and xviii 212 for the same distinction). Xenophon recommended a hipparch to procure for himself 'favourable orators' on the Council (Hipparch. i 8). Both Demosthenes and Aischines spoke of combinations between a general and a politician as a coalition of mutually complementary interests and skills (Dem. ii 29; [Dem.] xii 19; [Dem.] xiii 20; Aisch. iii 7). Isokrates criticized Timotheos for not troubling to make such alliances (xv 136), and Iphikrates' adlection of Kallistratos as his colleague in 372 probably had just this motive, though Xenophon failed to see it (Hell. vi 2, 39). Some other such combinations can indeed be detected: the link between the cousins Euboulos and Hegesileos (Dem. xix 290) may well be one, and the three brothers Aischines, Atrometos and Philochares may provide another (cf. Aisch. ii 149). Plutarch too had evidently received a clear impression of the dichotomy from his sources when he came to set the scene for Phokion's career (Phok. vii 5-6). Clearest of all is the fact that many leading fourth century politicians, indeed most of those who became prominent after 370, never became generals,[59] and their failure to do so must be reckoned a deliberate choice on their part.

This is to say, as compared with the political class of the sixth and earlier fifth centuries, the political class of the fourth and later fifth centuries gradually ceased to be closely linked with the generalship;

(59) E.G. Hypereides, Demosthenes, Lykourgos, Aischines, Demades, Euboulos, Stephanos, Diophantos, Androtion, Aristonikos, Kephalos, and both Polyeuktoi. Contrast, in the older generation, Archinos, Agyrrhios, Kallistratos, Aristophon, and both Thrasybouloi.

ceased to be the preserve of men of 'good family' or even of the rich;

ceased to engage in dynastic manoeuvring via political marriages; and

ceased to be an area within which families could develop long political

traditions. It needs to be explained both why these developments

occurred and why the last three failed to occur to the same extent in

the sphere of the military offices.

I think the answer must lie fundamentally in the nature of the

democratic power base. The earliest power bases, cult power and

ostentatious expenditure, had one thing in common. Just because great

wealth could be inherited and required no especial skill for its

political deployment once the techniques had been established, the

families for which wealth formed the basis of their political claim could

compete on comparable terms with that very facet of cultic expression

which was both one of the essential characteristics of gentilician think-

ing and power[60] and its strongest sanction against change - its

inheritability. Both power-bases shared this fundamental characteristic.

In contrast, rhetorical, financial, and administrative ability is

inheritable not in the sense that property or a ceremonial or cultic

status can be handed down from father to son, but only in the far more in-

direct sense that a son may well manifest in a large or small degree his

father's capacities and inclinations. It is true, of course, that part of

the new power base - rhetorical technique - could be acquired with application

---

(60) Via kinship with a god or hero as his ἰθαγενεῖc (**straight descendants**).
   It might be valuable to examine the myths which bolstered such links
   in order to see what relationship their development bore to the
   political importance of gentilician thinking.

and intelligence, and this fact both accounts for the growth of
rhetorical instruction via the sophists and their hand books and then
via the more or less formalized instruction given by, e.g. Lysias,
Isokrates, or Isaios, and at the same time made the transition to the
new power base less abrupt, in that it was only those who were at least
moderately wealthy who could afford to pay for tuition. Even so, the
necessity for the acquisition, first of the requisite political and
administrative skills and experience and then, by the exercise of these
skills, of a position of public prominence and influence, was a very
different route - and one much harder and longer - than the inheritance
of unimpaired property or a ceremonial cultic position, of the immediate
status as a potential centre of public attraction which went with them, and
of the immediately available opportunities for the exercise of charis or
of cult-power.

The military offices had different exi gencies.

(i) In the first place, the skills required for successful command were
very much the same in the fourth century as they had been in the sixth, so
that there was no technological reason for transferring power to a different group of people. It is notable, and may well in a negative way
exemplify this, that Iphikrates, one of the only Athenian generals to
whom a military innovation of importance is credited, was also one of the
handful of generals known to have been the first in their families to
achieve public position and practically the only one known to have been
acutely self-conscious of his humble social origins.[61]

(ii) In the second place, it might be worth hazarding the guess that when
it came to giving and obeying orders the average Athenian soldier or sailor

_____

(61) See APF 7737. Similarly, Phormion may be another novus homo, but
     this is ex silentio and the silence of our sources means virtually
     nothing.

preferred to take his orders from his social superiors rather than from his equals or inferiors, and that, other things being equal, they were not totally emancipated from the habit of mind which the Akarnanians manifested in 428 when they asked Athens to send them a son or relative of Phormion as his successor at Naupaktos (Thuc. iii 7, 1). It was evidently so when the Old Oligarch was writing ([Xen.] Ath.Pol. i 3), and though Eupolis in 422 and 412, and Aristophanes in 405,[62] had occasion to complain bitterly how Athens was currently electing 'worthless refuse' (καθάρματα   ) as generals instead of gentlemen, the old pattern evidently returned in the fourth century. Demosthenes' remark that the social background of Aischines and his brothers was such as to 'merit no dishonour, but not to merit the generalship either'(οὐδεμίας κακίας...ἀλλ' οὐδὲ cτρατηγίας γ' ἀξία; Dem. xix 237) is ad hominem, admittedly, but ought not to have been too much at variance with the prejudices of his audience, and a contemporary of his, instancing the case of a man executed for embezzlement, emphasized his status 'as a fellow-citizen of yours whose father has held the generalship'.[63]

(iii) In the third place, there was a real economic motive for choosing generals from among the propertied class. It was a valuable asset for a general to be able to assist the finances of a campaign or expedition by means of subventions from his own pocket, and this was particularly true in the fourth century when public finances tended to be so precarious. The classic exemplification of this is probably Timotheos' desperate efforts to save the expedition of 373, but Demosthenes had occasion to

---

(62) Eupolis F 117, I 288 K, and F 205, I 314 K; Ar. Frogs 725-733.

(63) [Dem.] xxxiv 50. It is tantalizing to have no clue to the family.

instance similar subventions by Nausikles, Diotimos, and Charidemos, and

the speaker of Lysias xix claimed that Aristophanes had been similarly

liberal with his own money in financing the expedition to Kypros in 390.[64]

A general who was generous of his own resources in this way might reason-

ably hope to recoup himself in booty from a successful campaign, and the

fact that its chances of success had been increased by his subventions both

increased his efficiency as a public servant and at the same time gave him

a legitimate claim on the future charis of an electorate.[65] Xenophon

brought the point out very clearly when he depicted the disgruntlement of

Nikomachides at being beaten for general by the rich businessman

Antisthenes. Sokrates was thereupon made to observe that, in addition to

his disciplinary and diplomatic duties, the general was expected to be 'in

a position to be able to provide necessary supplies for the soldiers'

(τοῖς στρατιώταις ἱκανὸς .... τὰ ἐπιτήδεια πορίζειν);

Antisthenes could be expected to spend (δαπανᾶν   ) for the sake of his

City's victory over enemies even more willingly than he had done for the

sake of his tribe's victory over its competitors, and that he would be a

---

(64) Dem. xlix 6-8 and particularly 11; Dem. xviii 114; Lys. xix 22.

(65) Nausikles, Diotimos, and Charidemos all received crowns for their

donations (Dem. xviii 114), and some of the crowns awarded to

Isokrates' pupils for subventions to the City (Isok. xv 93-94) may

well have been to them as generals. Cf. also Lyk. Leokr. 139

(quoted above, p. 94): "To earn your charis (a man) must ......

(e.g.) have subscribed generously from his own property for the

public safety."

a good leader if, having seen what was necessary, he is in a position to be able to provide it (Xen.Mem. iii 4,2 and 5-6). That the recruiting field for the generalship was so much the propertied class is no accident, and it should hardly be necessary to point out that to say that the recruiting field for the generalship was restricted because the major military offices received no salary is an illegitimate argument. Had there been effective pressure to widen the field, salaries would easily have been forthcoming.

The upshot of this argument is that property-power was real but limited. It was real in that the enlarged sphere of choice with which property-ownership on a large scale provided its owner could be used by him as a basis for influence in public life in three ways. (a) It could be a negative political sanction; (b) it could be deployed via energetic ambition as a claim for forensic charis; or (c) it could be deployed, via ambition and ostentatious expenditure, as a claim for political charis or as evidence of ability and willingness to support the responsibilities of the higher military offices. It was limited in that the first two techniques were open to logical or moral criticism and operated either negatively or at a sub-political level, while third, the only one of the techniques which could help positively in a political career, was the exploitation of a power-base to which, at various times during the period covered by the Register, there were several possible, and sometimes more effective, alternatives. Large-scale wealth as a power-base had had to establish itself in the sixth century against cult-power in its various forms, and was itself partly superseded by the end of the fifth century by political skills more appropriate to democratic pressures and democratic institutions.

Obviously this picture of the Athenian power-structure through three centuries is a gross schematization, open to innumerable qualifications.

It is not to be supposed, for example, that oratorical skill was a
completely valueless political asset before 460, while the racing victories
of Demades and Demetrios and the contemporary renaissance in privately
financed public works (p. 91 above) strongly suggest that in the 320's
the basis of a renewed appeal for major political power via ostentatious
expenditure lay not very far below the surface of Athenian society. Yet
I think it may be offered as a fair characterization. If we are prepared
to accept that the techniques of property-power were never valueless at
Athens and hardly ever if at all all-powerful, our model of the Athenian
power-structure can become at once more complex and more interesting: it
will also, I believe, approach more closely to the truth.

APPENDIX I

The diadikasia-documents

The diadikasia-documents[1] are currently taken to record changes
in the composition of the liturgical class in the years round 380. I
believe this explanation to be wrong, and that an alternative explanation is available which places the men named on them into an economic
category much more closely approaching that of the Periandric 1200 than
the narrow liturgical class proper of 300 or 400.

These documents form a group because (a) each of them is a list of
names, entered in the formula 'B instead of A', and (b) they all date
from the years round 380 B.C. According to the current view,[2] they
record the results of diadikasiai which took place in order to determine
which of two people was to be held liable to certain liturgies. From
the find-spot of $ii^2$1928, the Theatre of Dionysos, it was inferred that
$ii^2$1928 was a record of diadikasiai concerning the choregia: from the
two peculiarities of $ii^2$1932, its arrangement by deme and the appearance
of cult-heroes three times in the 'B'-position, it was inferred that it
was a record concerning the proeisphora. The other documents were referred
to the trierarchy. Consequently, these documents appear in both editions
of Inscriptiones Graecae under the rubric 'Catalogi iudiciales ad liturgias
pertinentes'. To date, only Goligher[3] has expressed doubts about this

---

(1) IG $ii^2$1928-1932; EM 12920 = Hesperia 7 (1938) 277 no.12; EM 12923 =
     Hesperia 7(1938) 306 no. 29; Agora I 4689 = Hesperia 15(1946) 160 no.17.

(2) Put forward by U. Köhler, AM 7(1882) 96-102, amended by Lipsius 1905-1915,
     593 note 14, and summarized by Kirchner in his note to $ii^2$1928.

(3) Hermathena 14 (1907) 503f.

interpretation. Nevertheless, it involves several major difficulties.

I. It was observed by Lewis (1954, 37) that EM 12923 is part of ii^{2}1928. Since ii^{2}1928 was found in the Theatre, while EM 12923 was found on the North Slope of the Akropolis, by far the most economical assumption is that the inscription was originally put up on the Akropolis, and that after it had been broken one fragment fell (or was taken) down the south side into the Theatre, while another much smaller piece fell (or was taken) down the North Slope.[4] Consequently, nothing can be inferred, from the find-spot of ii^{2}1928 in the Theatre, concerning the purpose for which the inscription was set up. Any attribution to the choregia must rely on other, more positive, evidence.

II. The preserved archon-dates in the surviving fragments are 383/2, 381/0 and 380/79,[5] and the three undated inscriptions (ii^{2}1928, 1929, 1932) all belong epigraphically and prosopographically in this same period. Since the thoroughness of excavations on and around the Akropolis has been such that the chances of a large number of these lists remaining undiscovered are very small indeed, it is probable either that we already possess a large proportion of those documents of this group which ever existed on stone, or that there were other such lists, but they were not put on stone. The latter possibility cannot be excluded outright, but can at least be rendered unlikely. It is beyond much doubt that diadikasiai in relation to the liturgies, of a kind which could be recorded by the formula used in these

---

(4) Cf. O. Broneer, Hesperia 7 (1938) 164, and compare the scatter of inscriptions originally set up in the hieron of Pandion, the find-spots of which are listed by Lewis 1955, 22-23.

(5) ii^{2}1930, line 2 and ii^{2}1931, line 3 ; Agora I 4689, line 3; ibid., line 2.

lists,[6] were part of Athenian legal life from the time of the Archidamian War and probably before, down to the 320's. ([Xen.] Ath.Pol. iii 4; Ath.Pol. lxi 1). If the current view is correct, it is exceedingly odd that records of the results of legal proceedings of this kind should have been deemed of sufficient importance to be put on stone only during what appears to have been a comparatively brief period at the end of the 380's and the beginning of the 370's. All the more odd is this when it is borne in mind that this is a period from which other public documents are not preserved in anything like the profusion in which they survive from the last thirty years of the fifth century or the forty years from 360 to 320. If the current view is to be maintained, at the very least it would be desirable to posit, and to provide evidence for, some specific legislative or administrative act, which continued in force only for a brief period and in terms of which this series of documents might make sense. However, immediately we posit such an act, the legal context of these documents becomes significantly different from that which would be the case if they merely recorded the normal kind of liturgical diadikasiai. That is to say, the very supposition which seems to be required in order to save the current view and to allow the surviving documents to be regarded as a small portion of a long series the majority of the members of which were not inscribed, at the same time makes them in some respect different from the rest of the hypothetical series. It is very much simpler not to postulate this hypothetical series, and to conclude instead that we possess

---

(6) The qualification is important. Such a formula could only be used to describe suits between individual persons, not skepseis, antidoseis, or diadikasiai with the naval authorities. If these latter were to be taken into account, the record would be virtually continuous.

already a large proportion of those documents of this group which ever existed, and that they are products of a legal context which continued in force only for a limited period of time.

III The margins of four of the surviving inscriptions[7] were so dressed as to provide a smooth surface for a neat join with another block of stone placed by the side. Concomitantly, the formulaic entries were allowed by the inscriber to overflow from the right-hand column of one block onto the left-hand part of the next block.[8] These facts prove nothing in themselves, but assume importance because of the curious format of Agora I 4689, which has an archon-date of 380/79 inscribed in large letters as a main heading, and the archon-date for the immediately preceding year, 381/0, inscribed just below in smaller letters as a subheading. Taken in conjunction with the virtual certainty that another stone adjoined on the left, this suggests strongly that the monument of which Agora I 4689 was a part contained lists for several years before, and perhaps including, 380/79, and that the whole was inscribed in the latter year as one unit. In some sense 380/79 may well be a terminal year, and this consorts ill with the supposition that these inscriptions record decisions of a kind that went on being made from the 420's to the 320's.

IV It has long been noted that ii^{2}1932, with its entries arranged under demotics as headings, has a different format from the others, but it has not apparently been noticed that since the three names on the fragmentary left-hand column of ii^{2}1928 also lack a demotic, the format of this column was the same as that of ii^{2}1932. Consequently, if ii^{2}1932 is to be referred

---

(7) ii^{2}1928, 1929, 1932, and Agora I 4689 (see Lewis 1954, 37).

(8) Cf. the left-hand column of ii^{2}1928; ii^{2}1929, line 12 (not obvious in ii^2, but clear enough from IG II 946); ii^{2}1932; Agora I 4689, line 2.

to the proeisphora on account of its format, the same must also be true for the left-hand column of ii^{2}1928.

To refer these two lists arranged by deme to the proeisphora as it functioned in the later fourth century is formally impossible. In terms of De Ste Croix's analysis of the proeisphora and the symmory-system (De Ste Croix 1953), the proeisphora functioned within, and in terms of, the symmory-system of eisphora organization, and Philochoros says flatly (FGH 328 F41) that the symmories were first introduced in 378/7. The attempt of Thomsen 1964, 114f., to impugn this statment involves (a) an unjustified suspicion of the word 'first' (πρῶτον) in Harpokration's quotation of Philochoros, and (b) an interpretation of Pollux viii 130 which entails the assumption that eisphorai always raised exactly 200 tal., which is certainly mistaken (cf. Ar. Ekkl. 823-825).

Either, then, both the lists in question must be dated after 377, or they do not refer to the proeisphora, functioning through symmories, as we understand it to have operated after that year. Since there is no cause for separating these two lists chronologically from all the others and for asserting that they alone of the group are to be dated after 377, they are not to be referred to the proeisphora. If they refer to the eisphora at all - which I shall argue is probable - we are to think in terms of an eisphora organized differently and superseded in 378/7 by what has come to be regarded as the typical fourth-century system of symmories.

One further minor difficulty might be thought to arise on the current view: could the three sanctuaries listed through their patron heroes (ii^{2}1932, lines 2-4) be proeispherontes? I doubt if this problem is a real one. Cult properties were certainly liable later on to the eisphora

(cf. ii^{2}1241, lines 14-17; ii^{2}2499, lines 37-39), as were deme properties
(ii^{2}2498) and at least in the fifth century some sanctuaries were rich
enough to count their reserves in terms of talents (cf. i^{2}310). Since
the proeisphora involved no personal executive responsibility, there
appears to be no good reason why sanctuaries, acting through their priests,
should not have been proeispherontes. One may even without absurdity
compare the fifth-century role of Athene as proeispherousa on a national
scale.

For these four reasons the current view of these documents cannot
be correct. A re-examination of the kind of decisions recorded in them
suggests another solution.

The diadikasia consisted of a hearing in court, between individuals
or between an individual and a group or between groups, where the court
was required to adjudicate between the two parties on a disputed claim
to a privilege or to an exemption from a liability. Naturally, decisions
thus made were not always of political importance and even less often of
administrative importance: Lipsius (1905-1915, 590f.) made what on his
classification was a correct decision in putting diadikasiai among the
'Privatklagen'. Yet these inscriptions are assuredly public documents,
a conclusion put beyond doubt both by the archon-dates and by the phrase
'κατὰ τὸ τῶ δήμο [ψήφισμα]' ' in ii^{2}1928, line 3. The field
of diadikasiai-decisions which are likely to be publicly so recorded is
very limited, and is rendered still more limited by four further considerations.

1. If ii^{2}1932 records the same kind of decision as the other documents
in the series, then the decisions so recorded must have been such that
cult-heroes and individuals were engaging in a judicial process on equal
terms. This fact immediately rules out any kind of liturgy, or other

duty, or any privileged position, requiring personal service and
activity.

2. The absence from the formula of any explanatory detail entails that
this formula conveyed sufficient information by itself for the purposes
of all concerned, including the State. This immediately excludes any
suggestion that the formula could have recorded a _diadikasia_ concerning
a change in the ownership of property. First, there was no reason why
such changes should have been a matter for public notice unless something
of public interest depended on them. Secondly, and quite apart from this,
it was the invariable custom at Athens, whenever a change in the ownership
of property was described in a public document, for the property concerned
to be given a specific description and (in the case of real property) its
location described with as much accuracy as was necessary. One may
compare, for example, the descriptions of real property given in the
"Attic Stelai",[9] in the fourth-century mining-leases and public sale
records,[10] and the hekatoste-records:[11] or, with property other than
land, the exact descriptions of slaves given in the manumission-lists.[12]
No such descriptions are to be found in the _diadikasia_-documents.

3. The simple formula 'B instead of A' conveys sufficient information
only if all the A's were already listed somewhere else; that is to say,
only if there was a publicly displayed list, a place on which was the
point at issue in the diadikasia. One corollary follows. Simply because

(9) W.K. Pritchett, _Hesperia_ 22 (1953) 225-299 and _Hesperia_ 30 (1961)
     23-29.

(10) ii^{2}1579 and 1581-1589; M. Crosby, _Hesperia_ 19 (1950) 189-312 and
     Hesperia 26 (1957) 1-23.

(11) ii^{2}1580 and 1594-1603; W. Peek, _AM_ 67(1942) 17-20 nos. 15-23;
     Lewis 1973, 187ff.

(12) ii^{2}1553-1578; Lewis 1959, 208ff; Lewis 1968, 368ff.

its composition was continually changing, there was no point in carving
this logically primary list on stone. I would imagine that the latter
was written up 'on whitewashed wooden boards' (ἐν σάνισι λελευκωμένοις)
like so many Athenian public documents, or on a pinax such as that used
by the deme of Otryna ([Dem.] xliv 35). Hence, of course, the primary
list has quite disappeared.

4. The simple formula 'B instead of A' makes sense only if there was
a fixed and constant number of A's, i.e. if the primary list had a
fixed and constant number of members.

These four considerations leave us with a fairly stringent set of
specifications. We have the following: that the decisions recorded
concern changes in the membership of a schedule of names or of property-
units; that this schedule had a fixed number of members; that this
schedule formed a publicly recognized and constituted body, the members
of which were liable to some impost or entitled to some privilege; that
changes in the constitution of this schedule were effected annually by
the legal procedure of diadikasia; and that the annual changes in its
composition were advertized in a permanent public list.

Obviously, this is very much the generalized case of the current
view. The point at issue is whether the particularization of it made
by Köhler is the only possible one. I think not.

There does exist a notice pertaining to a schedule which formed part
of Athenian life during parts of the working lifetimes of Lysias and
Isaios, but of which nothing is heard either earlier or later. This is
the body called the Thousand, our sole information for whom comes from
Harpokration s.v. Χίλιοι διακόσιοι   After briefly describing the
Periandric 1200, he goes on: "but Lysias in the speech 'Against Kleinias'
and Isaios in 'Supporting plea on behalf of Nikias' used the rounded-off
number, calling them the Thousand" (Λυσίας δ' ἐν τῷ πρὸς Κλεινίαν

(F 54 Thal.) καὶ Ἰσαῖος ἐν τῇ ὑπὲρ Νικίου συνηγορίᾳ (XXXIII Thal.) τῷ ἀπηρτισμένῳ ἀριθμῷ ἐχρήσαντο, χιλίους εἰπόντες).

No convincing explanation has yet been offered for the Thousand, and the context in which they appeared in the speeches of Lysias and Isaios quoted by Harpokration is unknown. It is extremely improbable that Harpokration was right in thinking that the two orators were merely using round figures to refer to the 1200 who comprised the trierarchical symmories. In the first place, the 1200 were certainly a creation of Periandros' law of 357, and Lysias' working lifetime is universally supposed to have come to an end soon after 380.[13] Secondly, when orators such as Demosthenes and Isaios wished to refer to the 1200, they used the proper figure, as we would expect them to do (Dem. xiv 16; Isaios F 18 Thal.). This was not a matter over which it was in a client's or a politician's interest to be vague. Yet it is perhaps permissible to infer from Harpokration's note (i) that the Thousand were not given a clear and unambiguous definition in the speeches, and (ii) that in the speeches there was nothing to distinguish them clearly from the 1200. This still leaves the field fairly open, but should at least exclude K.F. Hermann's suggestion that the Thousand were cavalrymen,[14]/while permitting the inference that at the date at which the speeches were delivered meaning of the phrase 'the Thousand' would be well enough known to the jury for no further comment to be required by the speaker. This is about all that can be teased out of Harpokration's note. On the other hand we have in the diadikasia-documents a series of decisions concerning membership of a schedule

---

(13) Blass I²344; Plöbst, RE 13 (1927) 2533-2534. [Dem.] lix 22 refers to
    a context of 380.

(14) De equitibus Atheniensibus 38. I know this reference only from
    Dindorf's edition of Harpokration, I p. 305 note.

of persons or property-units, the number of which was already fixed;
the point at issue seems to have been a disputed liability to an
impost or a privilege of public importance; and at least some of these
documents are dated in the years 383/2 - 380/79. I think we can with
profit place these documents in close association with the Thousand, and
regard the Thousand as the name for, and the size of, the schedule of
persons or properties membership of which was the point at issue in the
diadikasiai. It was argued above that these documents were the product
of a short-lived legal context, and the same seems to have been true of
the Thousand; and the two contexts appear to have been closely contemporary. Equally, though there is no obviously and certainly complete surviving list, [15] the number of changes recorded per year on these documents, ranging from at least 31 in ii^{2}1929 down to at least 10 in ii^{2}1932,
column II, requires that the logically primary list was of considerable
size. Though there is little point in speculating how many changes per
year there are likely to have been in a list of 1000 citizens or properties - whether from death or from loss of capital or civic status in
the case of citizens, or from changes of ownership in the case of properties - such figures as there are on the diadikasia-documents (which
are in any case minima) are consistent with the supposition that the
primary list had a thousand members.

This identification cannot be proved, and what follows has only
speculative value. Nevertheless two lines of approach help to indicate
a context into which the Thousand would fit and which would also be
consistent with the diadikasia-documents.

---

(15) ii^{2}1930, lines 3-26, might be a complete annual list, with 12 entries.
However, if, as Stschoukareff conjectured (AM 12 (1887) 134) and as
appears very probable, the lost ii^{2}1931 was a second copy of ii^{2}1930,
then there were many more entries for the year.

(F 54 Thal.) καὶ Ἰcαῖος ἐν τῇ ὑπὲρ Νικίου cυνηγορίᾳ
(XXXIII Thal.) τῷ ἀπηρτιcμένῳ ἀριθμῷ ἐχρήcαντο, χιλίουc
εἰπόντεc).

A.   The first is the well-known and much-discussed passage of [Demosthenes]
1 8-9. A propos of the expedition of September 362, Apollodoros says:
"Not only, gentlemen, did I have to pay the expenses at that time for
my trierarchy - which were heavy enough -, but I also paid in proeisphora,
including on this list both members of the deme and people from other
demes who owned property in the deme: my name was put on the list in
each of three demes, because my property was unconcealed. Waiving my
claim to exemption on the ground that I was acting as trierarch and that
I could not perform two liturgies, either physically or legally, I was
the first to deposit the proeisphora. I was unable to recover from others
the advances I had made on their behalf, because I was away serving you as
trierarch, and on my return I found that the sources which could have
indemnified me had been taken first by others, and only the insolvent
sources were left."

The problem has been to explain why there is no word about the
symmories or about the Three Hundred of Isaios vi 60, and why a special
procedure seems to have been adopted (Böckh 1886, I 620). An answer to
this is available: first briefly sketched by Lipsius 1905-15, 591 note 7,
it illuminates a good deal more than the mere predicament of Apollodoros.
I suspect that Apollodoros was correct in his statements that the proeisphora
was a liturgy and that there was a legal prohibition on the performance of
two liturgies concurrently, but deliberately misleading in his statement
that the procedure of September 362 was a proeisphora. I suggest also that
the procedure of 362 was deliberately differentiated from the "normal"
proeisphora, specifically in order that the exemption rule against two
simultaneous liturgies could not operate. For the probability is high
(we may fairly say) that if any known group of persons was concerned in
the proeisphora, that group would have been Isaios' Three Hundred.
Consequently there will have been a very high degree of identity between
the group of persons who were on the list of trierarchs, and the group of

persons who were concerned in the proeisphora (= members of the Three
Hundred): whichever of the two groups was the larger must have included
all or nearly all the members of the other. Hence, since the principal
occasions for the levying of eisphora, and therefore also of proeisphora,
were the equipping and despatch of navel expeditions such as the one
voted in September 362 (De Ste Croix 1953, 50), the operation of the two
exemption rules (i) against two sumultaneous liturgies and (ii) against
being obliged to perform a second liturgy until one or two years had
elapsed after a previous one (Dem. xx 8; Isaios vii 38) would have
allowed a very large proportion of potential trierarchs-cum-proeispherontes,
given sufficient ill-will, to contract themselves out of service whether
as trierarchs or as proeispherontes. Since moreover service as trierarch
presumably had priority in any case of conflict, the incidence of any major
naval expedition, such as that of September 362, would tend to reduce the
Three Hundred proeispherontes to a useless rump, from which the generals
and the apostoleis could extract no ready money of any consequence or
usefulness, at the very moment when it was wanted most.

Such a situation hamstrung the process of getting a fleet off to sea.
It was this situation which I think was circumvented by the special procedure of 362. Its author was surely Aristophon. That he was responsible
for the sending-out of the expedition is explicitly said by Apollodoros,
and the provision that the levy of man-power should be carried out through
the demarchs and the Councillors is in itself so notable a departure from
the usual procedure that when one finds the identical machinery being used
on the same occasion for the concomitant levy of money the conclusion that
the same man engineered both is unavoidable. It is worth noting two other
occasions on which Aristophon is known to have supported or proposed measures
aimed at blocking loop-holes in the financial administration, viz. his
support of the law of Leptines against exemptions and his decree to secure

the surrender of public moneys, both in 354.[16]

By enjoining in his decree that the levy of money, as of men, should be done through the demes, Aristophon very cleverly did two things at once. By by-passing the symmories (De Ste Croix 1953, 60) he thereby rendered the exemption laws ineffective; at the same time he obtained a list of de facto proeispherontes which was selected by local men whose knowledge cannot but have been exact and up to date. Given that some kind of proeispherontic procedure already existed before 362 (which from Isaios vi must be the case), Aristophon's procedure could at a pinch be described by Apollodoros as a proeisphora. He can have done so either loosely and honestly, with no intent to deceive, or - as I think more probable - deliberately and with intent to influence the jury in his favour by giving himself credit for his philotimia which he did not really deserve to receive. Aristophon, for his part, deserves much credit for realizing the crippling defect of the proeisphora-system as constituted in 362, and for successfully circumventing it on one partic- ular occasion: but his procedure did not, so far as we know, amount to a permanent legislative reform. One may be permitted to guess why. Aristophon cannot have been much less than 70 years of age in 362. He had been active in politics ever since 403 and perhaps before, but in spite of his Boiotian sympathies he has left so little trace in the record of Athenian politics in the 370's that it is fair to suppose him to have been out of sympathy with the reforming and expansionist policies of the period as represented for us by Aristoteles and Kallistratos. The lack of constructive long-range economic thinking shown on this occasion combines with the likelihood that Aristophon's concepts of economic administration had been crystallized long before 362 to suggest that we should bear in mind the possibility that Aristophon in 362 was authorizing

(16) Dem. xx 146; Dem. xxiv 11. For the date, Schäfer I²180, note 1.

a temporary return to an older system of eisphora-collection, a system
which predated the symmories.

B. We know from Philochoros (FGH 328 F41) that the eisphora-symmories
were established in 378/7. We know from Polybios (ii 62, 7) that in the
same year the timema of Attika was 5750 talents. It is almost certain
that these two statements are connected, both historically and historiographically: historiographically, in that the most likely source of
Polybios' information is Philochoros, the latest in time and the most
comprehensive of the Atthidographers, and a standard authority on most
Athenian legislative history: historically, in that it was the re-
assessment of the timema which provided the factual basis of up-to-date
property-values in terms of which the properties liable to the eisphora
could be equitably distributed among the new symmories. So, in 378/7 (a)
there was a re-assessment of taxable property, and (b) there was a new
division of the taxable property into new administrative units. However,
there were eisphorai throughout the Peloponnesian War and before, and in
the 390's eisphora was levied on a timema which included the values of
slaves (ML 58 B , lines 16-17; Isokr. xvii 49). Hence one asks, What
was new about the assessment of 378/7; why did the symmory-system come
into existence; and what system did it supersede?

Eisphora was levied on property. One could most naturally expect
that, at any rate at a time when most property was in land or physical
objects such as slaves, the machinery for the collection of eisphora
would be local; and the obvious people to do this administrative job
on the local level are the demarchs. The evidence that the demarchs
did perform local financial   administration during the fifth century
on behalf of the central government is quite clear and unambiguous.

1. The best evidence is i^{2}76 (= ML 73), the decree concerning the
first-fruits to be sent to Eleusis. The first section of this decree
(lines 4-21) enjoin, inter alia, that the demarchs are to select the
first-fruits and to send them to Eleusis.

2. IG i^{2}79, a fragmentary decree not closely datable (Meri t 1962, 25ff.)
contains provisions for a public levy to raise money for something to do
with the cult of Apollo. Lines 5-6 enjoin that the demarchs should exact
the money from those enrolled on the deme register.

In both these cases demarchs are acting as financial administration
on the local level, in a way exactly analogous to that which we would have
to posit for them if they were the local administrative officers for the
eisphora. In the absence of any other known machinery, the probability
that demarchs were the local collectors of eisphora-levies is, I believe,
very high.[17] This principle of the local collection of eisphora may
even go right back into the sixth century. One is reluctant to use
naukraries to prove anything,but it can hardly be denied that one of the
functions of naukraries was the raising of money for military, particularly naval, purposes; there is a persistent tradition (Hesychios s.v.
ναύκληροι ; An. Bekk. I 275. 20) that naukraries were local
divisions in some sense;. and there is Aristotle's explicit statement
that the demarchs took over the functions previously performed by the
naukraroi (Ath.Pol. xxi 5). Since, according to Aristotle, these
functions were 'aimed at the eisphorai and at the expenses which arise'
(τεταγμέναι) πρός τε τὰς εἰςφόρας καὶ τὰς δαπάνας τὰς γιγνομένας)
(Ath.Pol. viii 3), he clearly thought that demarchs were the responsible
officers for the collection of eisphora after Kleisthenes.

---

(17) Cf. also Ar. Clouds 37 and schol. ad loc., but the demarch who was
biting Strepsiades could have been exacting a debt due to the deme
rather than to the state.

There are three perceptible reasons why the local collection of eisphora was superseded in 378/7. The first is the movement of population away from the place of residence of the direct male ancestor in 507. The evidence from the fourth century that people were tending more and more to live elsewhere than in the deme of their demotic is quite large; and the more this tendency developed, the more difficult it was for a demarch to extract money in a hurry from his demesmen in the way laid down, for example, in IG i^{2}79. The second reason is the physical dispersal of property, which by the fourth century was yielding property-units so diversified in space and character (see p. 52 ff. above) that no demarch, however conscientious, could reasonably be expected to keep an effective check on them. The third reason is the growth in importance of 'invisible property' (ἀφανὴς οὐσία). The denotation of this term is astonishingly irregular,[18] and it can never have been part of official Athenian legal terminology, but broadly and usually it covers interest-bearing investments in mines, ship-loans, or deposits in banks. By the end of the fifth century one known fortune, that of Diodotos (APF 3885), consisted almost entirely of such liquid assets, and they account for over one-third of the estate of Demosthenes the elder and for five-sevenths of that of Pasion (APF 3597, XIII, and 11672, VIII). No demarch could keep track on fortunes of this nature.

That is, the system of eisphora-collection based on the local units of the demes failed to accommodate itself to the changed economic pattern of the fourth and the later fifth centuries. Eventually, its complete breakdown was recognized, and it was replaced by the non-territorial

(18) See Gernet 1968, 405 ff., and D.M. MacDowell, Andokides on the Mysteries (Oxford, 1962) 146f.

symmory-system in 378/7; a system which preserved the idea of a large
number of smallish administrative units, rounding off the 150-odd demes
to 100 symmories, but which, by taking no account of the location of a
property, allowed all the scattered possessions of one man to be liable
only in one administrative unit.

I suggest that what we have in the Thousand and the diadikasia-
documents is evidence of the breakdown of the earlier local system. I
suggest that at some time in the 390's or 380's a schedule was drawn up
containing the names of 1000 properties from which eisphora was to be
levied directly, partly but not entirely superseding the local administration,
and that this system itself proved unsatisfactory as a half-way house.
Hence, it was itself superseded in 378/7 by a far more thorough-going
reorganization, in which the proeisphora was placed on a much smaller
number of persons, who could be more easily approached in a hurry by the
central administration than the uncomfortably large number of a thousand;
also the proeisphora was more closely approximated to a liturgy and made
open to the exemption rules. (It is probable that the latter provision,
being in the interests of the proeispherontes, was the price that the
reformers had to pay in order to secure the acquiescence of the future
proeispherontes in a system which, being based on an up-to-date assessment,
would press on them more heavily in any case.)

Such a suggestion makes sense of several things. It explains what
Aristophan was doing in 362 if we think that he was returning to the
system in force before 378, and asking the councillors and the demarchs
(note; demarchs) to draw up a list arranged by demes and comparable in
function, and may be also in size, the the old Thousand. It explains why
Apollodoros complained so bitterly that he was heavily burdened in 362
because his property was visible, and that he could not re-imburse himself

on his return, if we think that these were two of the faults of the earlier regime; first, that it did not effectively catch those whose property was 'invisible', and secondly, that the arrangements whereby the individual member of the Thousand got his money back were faulty. Again, it explains why Harpokration was unable to see much difference between the 1000 and the 1200, why there is no mention of the 1000 after 378, why the diadikasia-documents pertain to a limited period about 380, and why the series breaks off. It also partly explains the arrangement of ii^{2}1928 and 1932 by deme if we suppose that local units continued to function - as with the levy of 362 - as the bodies from which the proeispheron recouped himself, and that the decision was only taken later that persons who were on the schedule did not have to be replaced by people from the same deme. Lastly, and most important, it does help to explain the genesis of the symmory-system as it functioned after 378/7, and why a re-assessment of taxable property was associated with it.

APPENDIX II

Military officials down to 300 B.C.

[These lists have been brought up to date (1980) as far as possible from evidence known to me. The list of generals has been collated with that of Fornara 1971, but includes some names not listed by Fornara.] The left-hand column of these lists attempts to identify 'family houses' (οἶκοι)(p. 124 above) which can be seen on our present evidence to have provided at least two military officials. The reference numbers are here purely ad hoc and arbitrary. The central column records the known holders of each post, in chronological order of attestation (first attestation in the case of the generalship). The right-hand column assesses the correlation of those listed here with the men listed in APF. In this column 'A' indicates that the man in question is himself in the liturgical class, 'B' that he has relatives, ancestors, or descendants in that class, and 'C' that he has no known connection with the class. The numbers are those of APF entries.

I TAXIARCHS

—	Kratinos, of tribe Oineis, 432/1?(Kratinos F 460, I 130 K. For the suggested date see Gomme, HCT II 75, but the argument is frail.)	C
3	Lamachos (I) son of Xenophanes of Oe, 426/5 (Ar. Ach. 569 and 1073 ff., with Lewis 1961, 120)	C
—	Thorykion, 400's? (schol. Ar. Frogs 362)	C
—	Eukleides, of tribe Aiantis (AE 1955, 180 pinax 1, line 2bis)	C
—	Aristokrates (II) son of Skellias (II) of tribe Kekropis, 411 (Thuc. viii 92,4)	A: 1904
—	Amphilochos, of tribe Leontis, 409 (Agora XVII 23, line 110)	C
—	Python, of tribe Leontis, 409 (Agora XVII 23, line 112)	C
13	Laches ((II) of Aixone?), 394 (Lys. iii 45)	C

152

–	Nikomachides (of tribe Pandionis?), 390's or 380's (Xen. Mem. III 4,1). The suggestion that his tribe was Pandionis depends on identifying Antisthenes, his successful opponent for the generalship, with Antisthenes (I) of Kytherros (see 1194).	C
26	Mantitheos son of Mantias of Thorikos, 349/8 (Dem. xxxix 17)	B : 9667
–	Menites son of Menon of Kydathenaion, 349/8 (Aisch. ii 169–170, with Wilamowitz, Hermes 44 (1909) 459 ff. and Lewis 1955, 31)	C
–	Lost Name 10, 346/5 (ii² 3201)	A: D 10
–	Diaitos of Pambota[dai], second half of the fourth century (Hesperia 26 (1957) 206 no. 52)	C
–	Demophon of Erchia (ibid.)	C
–	[–]res of tribe Kekropis (ibid.)	C
–	L[– –] of M[arathon] (ibid.)	C
–	G[– –] of Ai[gilia] (ibid.)	C
–	Boularchos son of Aristoboulos of Phlya, 339/8 (ii² 1155, with Dinsmoor, Hesperia 23 (1954) 291 ff.)	C
–	Philokles (II) son of Ph[il]otheos of S[ouni]on, 333/2 (Hesperia 9 (1940) 59 no. 8, lines 21–22)	C
–	Prokleides of [Th]o[r]ai, ca. 330 (SEG III 116)	C

In addition, of the two men said to have been killed with Strombichides in 405/4, one, Dionysodoros (Lys. xiii passim), was either taxiarch or general, and another, Kalliades (Lys. xxx 14), may have been a taxiarch.

II PHYLARCHS

6	Menexenos son of Dikaiogenes (I) of Kydathenaion, 429 (Isaios v 42)	B : 3773
18	Dieitrephes of Skambonidai, by 415/14 (Ar. Birds 799, with MacDowell, CQ 59/15 (1965) 41 ff and Fornara 1971, 57, for	C

his demotic)

— Pythodoros, of tribe Hippothontis, 412? (i² 950, line 180)   C

— Orthoboulos of Kerameis, 395 (Lys. xvi 13)   C

— Antiphanes, of tribe Akamantis, 394/3 (ii² 5222)   C

— Theophon, by 370 (Isaios xi 42)   B : 2921

— [....]okle[s] son of [...]tios of Kedoi, 373/2 (Hesperia 8   C
(1939) 3 no.2. He and his seven colleagues may be either
phylarchs or taxiarchs.)

— [....]as son of [.....]imos of [Myrrhi]nous (ibid.)   C

— [An]timachos son of [- -] of Pele[kes] (ibid.)   C

— Theophilos son of Eua[ngelos]of Herm[os] (ibid.)   C

20 Thrasymedes son of Kal[1]istratos (II) of Acharnai (ibid.)   C

— Char[ide]m[os] son of [E]uni[k -] of tribe Hippothontis (ibid.) C

— Kleonymos son of Kleoxenos of Marathon (ibid.)   C

— Philinos son of [....]nes of [Anaphlys]tos (ibid.)   C

19 Demainetos son of Demeas of Paiania, mid fourth century (ii²   B : 3276
3130)

19 Demeas son of Demainetos of Paiania, mid fourth century (ibid.) B : 3276

19 Demosthenes son of Demainetos of Paiania, mid fourth century (ibid.) B:3276

— Anacharsis son of Me[- -], of ?Kydathenaion?, mid fourth   C
century (ii² 3135 and 3136). For his demotic cf. ii² 1576a,
lines 23-24, but cf. also ii² 134-137 with Ferguson, Klio 14
(1914-15) 394 note 3. See 12198.

— Kleophanes, 349/8 (Plut. Phok. xiii 6). The cavalry at Tamynai C
obeyed his orders, but he cannot have been hipparch because the
two hipparchs of the year are already known. Most likely he was
phylarch in this year.

— Euthykrates of Perg[ase], fourth century (Hesperia 9 (1940)   C
57 no. 6)

–	Moiragenes of Ika[ria] (ibid.)	C
–	[Ha]gnodoros of Pa[iania] (ibid.)	C
–	Pheidon, 350's or 340's (Mnesimachos F 4, line 7, II 437 K)	C
–	Lykophron, by ca. 340 (Hyp. ii (Lyk.) 17)	C
–	Demetrios son of [....]phanes of Alopeke, ca. 330 (SEG III 115)	C
–	[– ca.9 –]n of Oe, ca. 325 (Hesperia 15 (1946) 176 no. 24)	C
–	[– – –] of tribe Erechtheis, 322/1 (ii² 379, line 3, with Dinsmoor, Archons 27 for the date)	C

III HIPPARCHS

1	Lakedaimonios (son of Kimon (II) of Lakiadai), 450's or 440's (DAA 146 no. 135)	B:8429,XIII
–	Xenophon (son of Euripides of Melite)(ibid.)	B : 5951
–	Pronapes (son of Pronapides of Prasiai) (ibid.)	A : 12250
–	Simon, 425/4 (Ar. Knights 242-3 with schol.)	C
–	Panaitios, 425/4 (ibid.)	C
–	Pythodoros son of Epizelos of Halai Araphenides, ca.420 (i²816)	A: 12402
18	Dieitrephes of Skambonidai, by 415/14 (Ar. Birds 799 and 1442-3)	C
–	Kallistratos son of Empedos (I) of Oe, 413 (Paus. vii 16,5-6. [Plut.] Mor. 844 B has confused him with the orator Kallistratos and placed him in Aphidna, but his proper demotic is attested at ML 77, line 21)	C
–	Lysimachos, 404/3 (Xen. Hell. ii 4, 8 and 26)	C
26	Pamphilos of Keiriadai, ca. 395 (Lys. xv 5)	B : 9667
–	[–]kles of Erchia, between 375/4 and 370/69 (ii² 102, lines 18-19)	C
–	[Democh]ares of Paiania (ibid.)	A : 3737
–	Nike[....], by or in 368/7 (ii² 104, lines 1-2)	C
–	[....]ikles (ibid.)	C
–	Kephisodoros of Marathon, 363/2 (Ephoros, FGH 70 F 85, Paus.	C

viii 9, 10, Harp. s.v. Κηφισόδωρος)

- Antikrates son of Sokrates of Hermos, fourth century   C
  (Hesperia 22 (1953) 50-51)

- Patrokles son of Hierokles of Philaidai (ibid.)   C

- Meidias (I) son of Kephisodoros (I) of Anagyrous, 349/8   A : 9719
  (Dem. xxi 164, 166, 171, 173-4)

- Kratinos, 349/8 (Dem. xxi 132 with schol.)   C

- Pheidon of Thria, hipparch to Lemnos shortly after the middle   C
  of the fourth century (Kroll and Mitchel, Hesperia 49 (1980)
  89 ff.)

- Lykophron, hipparch to Lemnos for two years in the 330's   C
  (Hyp. ii (Lyk.) 17)

- Philokles son of Phormion of Eroiadai, three or four times   A: 14541
  by 325 (Dein. iii 12)

- [Eue]tion son of Pythangelos of Kephisia, ca. 325 (Hesperia 6   C : 5463
  (1937) 462 no. 10)

- Epilykos son of Nikostra[tos of Gargettos] (ibid.)   C : 8429,XVII

- Theogenes son of Theomedes of Eleusis, ca. 320 (ii² 1955,line 3) C

- Demetrios (I) son of Phanostratos of Phaleron, ca.320 (ii²2971)   A : 3455

- Lost Name 11, ca. 320? (ii² 3209)   A : D 11

- Antidoros of Thria, fourth century (Kroll and Mitchel,   C
  Hesperia 49 (1980) 92 f.)

- [- - son of - om]achos of Lamptra, second half of the fourth   C
  century or early third century (Hesperia 43 (1974) 312 no. 1).
  Vanderpool ad loc. suggests that he was a member of the Kineas-
  Nikomachos family (see 12883).

- [- - son of -]enes of Pro[spalta] or Pro[balinthos], late   C
  fourth or third century (Vanderpool, Hesperia 43 (1974) 313 no.2)

- [- - son of -]es of A[- -] (ibid.)   C

IV GENERALS

Repeated tenure of the office being the rule rather than the exception, full references to every generalship held by each man would overload this section without being immediately à propos. A PA reference is therefore deemed to be sufficient unless the evidence that a particular man held the generalship at all has appeared since PA. The dates given are those of first recorded tenure of the office. They are often approximate, and are inserted only for guidance : they should not be taken as necessarily reflecting any new interpretation of the evidence.

–	Melanthios son of Phalanthos, 499/8 (PA 9764 with Hesperia, Suppl. VIII 400 f. for his patronymic)	C
1	Miltiades (IV) son of Kimon (I) of Lakiadai, 490/89 (PA 10202)	B : 8429
16?	Aristeides (I) son of Lysimachos (I) of Alopeke, 490/89 (PA 1695)	B: 1695
–	Stesileos son of Thrasyleos, 490/89 (PA 12906)	C
–	? Polyzelos, 490/89 (PA 11957)	C
–	? Kynegeiros son of Euphorion (I) of Eleusis, 490/89 (Plut. Mor. 305 BC, but he also refers to Kallimachos, polemarch at Marathon, as a 'strategos')	C
–	Themistokles (I) son of Neokles (I) of Phrearrhioi, 481/0 (PA 6669)	A : 6669
2	Xanthippos (I) son of Ariphron (I) of Cholargos, 480/79 (PA 11169)	B:11811
–	Myronides son of Kallias, 479/8 (PA 10509)	C
–	Leokrates son of Stroibos, 479/8 (PA 9084)	C
1	Kimon (II) son of Miltiades (IV) of Lakiadai, 478/7 (PA 8429)	A : 8429
–	Lysistratos, 476/5 (PA 9591)	C
–	Lykourgos (of Boutadai?), 476/5 (PA 9246)	B?: 9251
–	Kratinos, 476/5 (PA 8750)	C
5	Leagros (I) son of Glaukon (I) of Kerameis, 465/4 (PA 9028)	B : 3027
22?	Ephialtes son of Sophonides, mid 460's? (PA 6157)	C

- Sophanes son of Eutychides of Dekeleia, 465/4 (PA 13409)   C

- Hippodamas ((I) of Agryle?), 460 or 459 (ML 33, line 63 : for   C
his demotic see M.K. Pope, Studies... Robinson (St. Louis, 1953)
II 1048)

- Ph[ryni]chos, of tribe Erechtheis, 460 or 459 (PA 15009, but   C
see ML 33, line 6 note)

6 Dikaiogenes (I) of Kydathenaion, 460 or 459 (PA 3773). For date   A : 3773
and status see Isaios v 42 and 3773, but unfortunately the words
'while serving as general' dropped out during printing from the
second line of the entry APF 3773.

- Charitimides, 459 (Ktesias, FGH 688 F 14, 37 (33))(in PA as   C
Charmantides, PA 15497)

2 Perikles (I) son of Xanthippos (I) of Cholargos, 457/6 (PA 11811) A:11811

9? Tolmides son of Tolmaios (of Anaphlystos?), 456/5 (PA 13879)   B?: 2724

- [Pyth?]odotos, of tribe [Hipp]othontis, 450's? (Hesperia 33   C
(1964) 21 no. 5, line 2)

27 Thoukydides (I) son of Melesias (I) of Alopeke,?444/3 (PA 7268,   B : 7268
claimed as general by Fornara 1971, 48, on the basis of anon.
vit. Thuc. 6)

- Sokrates (I) of Anagyrous, 441/0 (PA 13102)   A: 13102

- Sophokles (I) son of Sophillos of Kolonos, 441/0 (PA 12834)   C

- Kreon of Skambonidai, 441/0 (PA 8785)   C

5 Glaukon (II) son of Leagros (I) of Kerameis, 441/0 (PA 3027)   A : 3027

20 Kallistratos (I) of Acharnai, 441/0 (PA 8148)   C

- Xenophon son of Euripides of Melite, 441/0 (PA 11313)   B: 5951

- Glauketes? of Peiraieus?. 441/0 (PA 2951, with Jacoby's note on   C
Androtion, FGH 324 F 35, and Fornara 1971, 49)

- Kleitophon of Thorai, 441/0 (PA 8548)   C

- Thoukydides (son of Pantainetos of Gargettos?), 440/39 (PA 7272) C

8	Hagnon son of Nikias of Steiria, 440/39 (PA 171)	B : 7234
–	Antikles (of Melite?), 440/39 (PA 1051)	B?:10652
–	Tlepolemos, of tribe Aiantis, 440/39 (PA 13863)	C
–	Epiteles, 438 (PA 4953)	C
–	Dem[okleides], of tribe Aigeis, 439/8 (ML 56, line 28)	C
–	Ch[– 10 –], of tribe Leontis, 439/8 (ML 56, line 29)	C
–	[Leon], of tribe Antiochis, 439/8 (name restored by Andrewes and Lewis, JHS 77 (1957) 179, but left blank in ML 56, line 32)	C
21?	Menippos, 430's (PA 10033)	C
1?	Metiochos (II), 430's (com. adesp. 1325, III 629 K)	B :8429, XIV
12	Phormion son of Asopios (I) (of Paiania?), 430's (PA 14958, with Fornara 1971, 77 f. for his demotic)	C
3	Lamachos (I) son of Xenophanes of Oe, 430's (PA 8981)	C
–	Proteas son of Epikles of Aixone, 435/4 (PA 12298)	C
4	Diotimos (I) son of Strombichos (I) of Euonymon, 433/2 (PA 4386)	B : 4386
1	Lakedaimonios son of Kimon (II) of Lakiadai, 433/2 (PA 8965)	B : 8429
–	Metagenes of Koile, 433/2 (PA 10088)	B: 10088
–	Drakontides son of Leogoras of Thorai, 433/2 (PA 4551)	B?: 4551
10	Archestratos son of Lykomedes (of Phlya?), 433/2 (PA 2411)	B : 9238
–	Kallias son of Kalliades, 433/2 (PA 7827)	C : 9574
–	Archena[utes], 433/2 (i² 367, line 4 ; ATL III 331)	C
–	Sokrates son of Antigenes of Halai Araphenides, 432/1 (PA 13099)	C
–	Karkinos son of Xenotimos of Thorikos, 432/1 (PA 8254)	A : 8254
–	Kleopompos son of Kleinias (of Thria?), 432/1 (PA 8613)	C:600,VI
–	Eukrates (of Melite?), 432/1 (i² 296, line 5 : Fornara 1971, 76)	C
–	Hestiodoros son of Aristokleides, 430/29 (PA 5207)	C
–	Phanomachos son of Kallimachos, 430/29 (PA 14069)	C
–	Melesandros, 430/29 (PA 9803)	C
–	Kleippides son of Deinias of Acharnai, 429/8 (PA 8521)	C

11	Nikias (I) son of Nikeratos (I) of Kydantidai, 428/7 (PA 10808)	A: 10808
12	Asopios (II) son of Phormion (of Paiania?), 428/7 (PA 2669)	C
18	Nikostratos son of Dieitrephes of Skambonidai, 428/7 (PA 11011)	C
-	Lysikles, 428/7 (PA 9417)	C
-	Paches son of Epikouros, 428/7 (PA 11746)	C
-	Eurymedon son of Theokles (of Myrrhinous?), 427/6 (PA 5793)	B?: 8792,XI
13	Laches (I) son of Melanopos (I) of Aixone, 427/6 (PA 9019)	C
-	Demosthenes son of Alkisthenes (I) of Aphidna, 427/6 (PA 3585)	A : 3585
-	Prokles son of Theodoros, 427/6 (PA 12214)	C
-	Charoiades son of Euphiletos, 427/6 (PA 15529)	C
16	Hipponikos (II) son of Kallias (II) of Alopeke, 427/6? (PA 7658)	A:7826,IX
2	Hippokrates son of Ariphron (II) of Cholargos, 426/5 (PA 7640)	B : 11811
-	Aristoteles son of Timokrates of Thorai, 426/5 (PA 2055=2057, with Gomme, HCT II 417-18 and Lewis 1961, 121 f.)	C:828,VI
-	Hierophon son of Antimnestos, 426/5 (PA 7515)	C
-	Pythodoros son of Isolochos of Phlya, 426/5 (PA 12399)	C
-	Sophokles son of Sostratides, 426/5 (PA 12827)	C
-	Simonides, 426/5 (PA 12713)	C
-	Demodokos (I) of Anagyrous, 425/4 (PA 3464)	C
9?	Autokles (I) son of Tolmaios of Anaphlystos, 425/4 (PA 2724)	A : 2724
27	Thoukydides son of Oloros of Halimous, 424/3 (PA 7267)	A : 7268
-	Aristeides son of Archippos, 425/4 (PA 1685)	C : 1695
6	Kleon (I) son of Kleainetos (I) of Kydathenaion, 424/3 (PA 8674)	B : 8674
-	Eukles, 424/3 (PA 5704)	C
-	Symmachos, 423/2 (Diod. xii 72,3 : omitted from PA)	C
-	Euthydemos son of Eudemos, 422/1 (PA 5521)	C
-	Alkibiades (III) son of Kleinias (II) of Skambonidai, 420/19 (PA 600)	A:600,IX
-	Hyperbolos son of Antiphanes of Perithoidai, ca. 420 (PA 13910)	A: 13910

–	Kallistratos son of Empedos (I) of Oe, 418/17 (ML 77, line 21)	C
–	Rhinon son of Charikles of Paiania., 417/16 (PA 12532)	B : 2254
–	Teisias (II) son of Teisimachos of Kephale, 417/16 (PA 13470 = 13479)	A: 13479
10	Kleomedes son of Lykomedes (I) of Phlya, 417/16 (PA 8598)	B : 9238
–	Philokrates son of Demeas, 416/15 (PA 14585)	C
–	Laispodias of Koile, 415/14 (PA 8963, with Hesperia, Suppl. VIII 400 for his demotic)	C
–	Pythodoros son of Epizelos of Halai Araphenides, 415/14 (PA 12402 = 12410)	A: 12402
–	Telephonos, 415/14 (ML 77, line 63)	C
–	Demaratos, 415/14 (PA 3283)	C
18	Dieitrephes son of Nikostratos of Skambonidai, 414/13 (PA 3755)	C
15	Konon (II) son of Timotheos (I) of Anaphlystos, 414/13 (PA 8707)	A: 13700
–	Charikles son of Apollodoros, of tribe Oineis, 414/13 (PA 15407)	B: 13479
–	Euetion (of Sphettos?), 414/13 (PA 5460)	C : 5463
–	Menandros, 414/13 (PA 9857)	C
–	Aristokrates (II) son of Skellias (II) of tribe Kekropis, 413/12 (PA 1904)	A : 1904
21?	Hippokles son of Menippos, 413/12 (PA 7620)	C
–	Diphilos, 413/12 (PA 4464)	C
4	Strombichides (I) son of Diotimos (I) of Euonymon, 412/11 (PA 13016)	B : 4386
11	Eukrates son of Nikeratos (I) of Kydantidai, 412/11 (PA 5757)	A: 10808
–	Phrynichos son of Stratonides of Deiradiotai, 412/11 (PA 15011)	C
–	? Peisandros son of Glauketes of Acharnai, 412/11 (Nepos, Alc. 5)	C
–	Thrasykles, 412/11 (PA 7317)	C
–	Diomedon, 412/11 (PA 4065)	C
–	Euktemon, 412/11 (PA 5782)	C
–	Leon of Salamis, 412/11 (PA 9100, with Andrewes and Lewis, JHS	C

77 (1957) 179 note 10)

–	Onomakles, of tribe Kekropis , 412/11 (PA 11476)	C
–	Skironides, 412/11 (PA 12730, with Lewis 1961, 122)	C
–	Charminos, 412/11 (PA 15517)	C
8	Theramenes son of Hagnon of Steiria, 411 (PA 7234)	A : 7234
–	Aristarchos (of Dekeleia?), 411 (PA 1663)	C : 1663
–	Alexikles, 411 (PA 535)	C
–	Thymochares, 411 (PA 7406)	C: 13964
–	Melanthios, 411 (PA 9768)	C
10	Chaireas son of Archestratos (of Phlya), 411/10 (PA 15093)	B : 9238
–	Eumachos of Euonymon, 411/10 (Xen. Hell. i 1, 22; ML 84, line 35 ; Andrewes, JHS 73 (1953) 4 note 13 ; Fornara 1971, 68)	C
–	Thrasyllos, 411/10 (PA 7333)	C
–	Simichos, 411/10 (Hell. Ox. vii 4 Bart.; schol. Aisch. ii 31. The exact form of his name is not clear, and Thompson (Hesperia 36 (1967) 106–7) suggests that it is a corruption of Strombichides.)	C
–	Eukleides, 410/09 (ML 84, line 17)	C
11	Thrasyboulos son of Lykos of Steiria, 410/09 (PA 7310)	A : 7310
–	Anytos (I) son of Anthemion (I) of Euonymon, 410/09 (PA 1324)	B : 1324
–	Pasiphon of Phrearrhioi, 410/09 (PA 11668)	C
–	Oinobois of Dekeleia, 410/09 (PA 11357)	C
–	Dexikrates of Aigilia, 410/09 (PA 3226)	C
–	Theoros, of tribe Aiantis, 409 (PA 7223 with Hesperia 33 (1964) 43 no. 15, line 14)	C
–	Archestratos of Phrearrhioi, 409 (PA 2430, Fornara 1971, 69–70)	C
–	Diodoros, 409/8 (PA 3916)	C
–	Mantitheos, 409/8 (PA 9670)	C
–	Leotrophides, 409/8 (PA 9159). Pace Fornara 1971, 69, I see no reason why he should not be identified with the choregos Leotrophides referred to by Aristophanes in 414 (Birds 1405–7),	A**

who was omitted in error from APF.

–	Timarchos, 409/8 (PA 13623)	C
–	Adeimantos son of Leukolophides of Skambonidai, 408/7 (PA 202)	C
–	Phanosthenes of Andros, 407/6 (PA 14083 with M.B. Walbank, Hesperia 45 (1976) 289 ff. at 293)	C
2	Perikles (II) son of Perikles (I) of Cholargos, 407/6 (PA 11812)	B: 11811
–	Aristogenes, 407/6 (PA 1781)	C
–	Erasinides, 407/6 (PA 5021)	C
–	Lysias, 407/6 (PA 9351)	C
–	Protomachos, 407/6 (PA 12318)	C
–	Thrasylos, 406/5 (Fornara 1971, 70)	C
–	Diomedon, 406/5 (Fornara 1971, 70)	C
–	Philokles, 406/5 (PA 14517)	C
3	Tydeus (I) son of Lamachos of Oe, 405/4 (PA 13884)	C
–	? Kleophon son of Kleippides of Acharnai, 405/4 (schol. Ar. Frogs 679, with M.H. Jameson, TAPA 86 (1955) 86 ff., but also Lewis 1961, 123, and Fornara 1971, 70)	C
–	Kalliades, 405/4 (PA 7775)	C
–	? Dionysodoros, 405/4 (PA 4278 ; it is impossible to decide from Lysias xiii whether he was taxiarch or general in 405/4)	C
–	Kephisodotos, 405/4 (PA 8312)	C
–	Archinos of Koile, 404/3 (PA 2526)	C
–	Aisimos, 404/3 (PA 311)	C
–	Hieronymos, 395/4 (PA 7552)	C
–	Mnesikl[–], 394/3 (ii² 5521)	C
–	[Tho]ukle[ides], 394/3 (ii² 5521)	C
–	Ktesikles, 393/2 (PA 8861)	C
17	Iphikrates (I) son of Timotheos (I) of Rhamnous, 393/2 (PA 7737)	B : 7737

16	Kallias (III) son of Hipponikos (II) of Alopeke, 391/0 (PA 7826)	A : <u>7826</u>
4	Diotimos ((II) son of Olympiodoros (I) of Euonymon?), 390/89 (PA 4370)	B : <u>4386</u>
6	Chabrias son of Ktesippos (I) of Aixone, 390/89 (PA 15086)	A: <u>15086</u>
26	Pamphilos of Keiriadai, 390/89 (PA 11545)	B : <u>9667</u>
–	Ergokles, 390/89 (PA 5052)	A : <u>5052</u>
22?	Philokrates son of Ephialtes, 390/89 (PA 14596)	C
25	Kleoboulos son of Glaukos of Acharnai, 389/8 (PA 8558)	C
–	Demainetos, 389/8 (PA 3265)	C?: <u>3276</u>
23	Agyrrhios of Kollytos, 388/7 (PA 179)	B : <u>8157</u>
24	Thrasyboulos son of Thrason of Kollytos, 388/7 (PA 7305)	A : <u>7305</u>
–	Eunomos, 388/7 (PA 5861)	C
–	Dionysios, 387/6 (PA 4092)	C
–	Leontichos, 387/6 (PA 9036)	C
–	Phanias, 387/6 (PA 14009)	C
–	Antisthenes (I) son of Antiphates of Kytherros, after 380? (PA 1184 = 1194)	A : <u>1194</u>
–	Demophon, 379/8 (PA 3693)	C
–	Demeas, 379 (schol. Aristeides 3.281 Dind.)	C
23	Kallistratos (I.) son of Kallikrates (I) of Aphidna, 378/7 (PA 8157)	A : <u>8157</u>
15	Timotheos (II) son of Konon (II) of Anaphlystos, 378/7 (PA 13700)	A: <u>13700</u>
–	Kedon, 376/5 (PA 8281)	C
–	? Stesikles, 374/3 (Xen. Hell. vi 2, 10 : = PA 8861?)	C
4	Autokles (I) son of Strombichides (I) of Euonymon, 368/7 (PA 2727)	B : <u>4386</u>
12?	Phormion, 368/7 (PA 14950)	C
–	Spoudias, 368/7 (PA 12861)	C
–	Chares son of Theochares of Angele, 367/6 (PA 15292)	A: <u>15292</u>

23	Timomachos (II) of Acharnai, 367/6 (PA 13797)	B : <u>8157</u>
–	Lysistratos, 366/5 (PA 9598)	C
–	Alkimachos of Anagyrous, 364/3 (PA 616)	C
13	Laches (II) (son of Laches (I)?) of Aixone, 364/3 (PA 9018)	C
–	Ergophilos, 363/2 (PA 5062)	C
–	Kallisthenes, 363/2 (PA 8089)	C
–	Aristophon son of Aristophanes (I) of Azenia, 363/2 (PA 2108)	B : <u>2108</u>
–	Menon of Potamos, 362/1 (PA 10085)	C
7	Leosthenes (I) of Kephale, 362/1 (PA 9141)	B : <u>9142</u>
–	Hegesileos, 362/1 (PA 6339)	C
–	Theotimos, 361/0 (PA 7055)	C
–	Kephisodotos (of Acharnai?), 360/59 (PA 8313, with Anaxandrides, F 41, II 151 K, for his demotic)	C
26	Mantias son of Mantitheos (I) of Thorikos, 360/59 (PA 9667)	A : <u>9667</u>
–	Exekestides of Thorikos, 357/6 (PA 4718)	C?: <u>4718</u>
–	Philochares of Rhamnous, 357/6 (PA 14779)	C
–	Diokles (II) of Alopeke, 357/6 (PA 4015)	A : <u>4015</u>
17	Menestheus son of Iphikrates (I) of Rhamnous, 356/5 (PA 9988)	A : <u>7737</u>
13	Melanopos (II) son of Laches (I) of Aixone, 355/4 (PA 9788)	C
24	Thrasyboulos son of Thrason of Erchia, 353/2 (PA 7304)	B : <u>7305</u>
–	Nausikles son of Klearchos of Oe, 353/2 (PA 10552)	A: <u>10552</u>
–	Antiochos, 353/2 (PA 1154)	C
–	Athenodoros of Hestiaia, 352/1 (PA 270)	C
–	Charidemos son of Philoxenos of Acharnai, 351/0 (PA 15380)	A: <u>15380</u>
22?	Ephialtes, 350/49 (Philochoros, FGH 328 F 155)	C
6	Proxenos (II) son of Harmodios (III) of Aphidna, 349/8 (PA 12270)	A:<u>12267</u>
–	Phokion son of Phokos (I), 349/8 (PA 15076)	B: <u>15076</u>
–	Molottos son of Eunomos of Aphidna, 349/8 (PA 10403 = 10406)	C
14	Phaidros (I) son of Kallias (I) of Sphettos, 347/6 (PA 13964)	A: <u>13964</u>

25	Philochares son of Atrometos of Kothokidai, 345/4 (PA 14775)	B: 14625
-	Diopeithes (II) (son of Diphilos (I)) of Sounion, 343/2 (PA 4327)	B: 4487
-	Nikoteles, general to Samos, fourth century (Kroll and Mitchel, Hesperia 49 (1980) 91 f.)	C
-	Kephisophon (III) son of Kephalion (I) of Aphidna, 342/1 (PA 8410)	A:8410
-	[- 6 -]k[-], of tribe Oineis, 338? (Agora XVII 24)	C
4	Diotimos (III) son of Diopeithes (I) of Euonymon, 338/7 (PA 4384)	A:4386
-	Stratokles (of Lakiadai?), 338/7 (PA 12931, with Bradeen, Hesperia 33 (1964) 57 note 103 for the demotic)	C
-	Lysikles, 338/7 (PA 9422)	C
-	Deinokrates (II) son of Kleombrotos (I) of Acharnai, 336/5 (PA 3181 = 3185)	B : 9251
-	Philemonides, 330's (Hesperia, Suppl. VIII 274 line 3)	C
-	Sophilos son of Aristoteles of Phyle, 333/2 (Hesperia 9 (1940) 62 no. 8 col. ii, line 11)	C
15	Konon (III) son of Timotheos (II) of Anaphlystos, 333/2 (ibid., line 9)	A: 13700
-	Diphilos of Aixone, general to Samos 327/6 or 326/5 (ii² 1628, line 120 : Inschr. v. Priene 5 line 18. Cf. ii² 5429)	C
-	[- -]os of Eroiadai, genral to Samos 327/6 or 326/5 (ii² 1628, line 110)	C
-	Dioxandros, 326/5 (PA 4526)	C
-	Philokles son of Phormion of Eroiadai, 325/4 (PA 14521=14541)	A: 14541
6	Dikaiogenes (IV) son of Menexenos (II) of Kydathenaion, 324/3 (PA 3776)	B : 3773
7	Leosthenes (II) son of Leosthenes (I) of Kephale, 324/3 (PA 9142 = 9144)	A : 9142
-	Pherekleides son of Pherekles of Perithoidai, 324/3 (PA 14187)	C
-	Euetion (son of Pythangelos of Kephisia), 323/2 (PA 5462)	C : 5463

-     Antiphilos, 322/1 (PA 1264)   C

-     Charias son of Euthykrates of Kydathenaion, 322/1 (PA 15346)   A: 15346

14   Thymochares (I) son of Phaidros (I) of Sphettos, 322/1? (PA 7412) A:13964

-     Derkylos son of Autokles of Hagnous, 319/8 (PA 3249)   A : 3249

-     Aischetades, 318/7 (PA 322)   B: 11473

-     Demetrios (I) son of Phanostratos of Phaleron, 318/7 (PA 3455)   A : 3455

-     Aristoteles, 315/4 (PA 2054)   C

-     [- -]os of Teithras, 306/5 (ii^2 1487, line 83)   C

-     [-]l.des of Dekeleia, 306/5 (ii^2 1487, line 84)   C

-     Nikon, 306/5 (PA 11095)   C

-     Hegesias, 306/5 (PA 6314)   C

-     Demochares (II) son of Laches (I) of Leukonoion, 306/5 (PA 3716) B: 3716

-     Aristyllos, 306/5 (PA 2128)   C

-     S[- -], 306/5 (ii^2 1487, line 82)   C

4?   Olympiodoros ((II) son of Diotimos (III) of Euonymon?), 302/1   B : 4386

       (PA 11387 = 11388?)

-     [- - son of om]achos of Lamptra, second half of the fourth   C

       century or early third century (Hesperia 43 (1974) 312 no. 1).

       See also the hipparchs' list sub fin.

(Note that the generals from the klerouchies listed on ii^2 1672, lines 271-278 for 329/8 are not included in this list.)

APPENDIX   III

Athenian competitors in the four- and two-horse contests
at Panhellenic Games

Chronological order is observed as much as possible. All entries are for
the four-horse contests unless otherwise stated.

1.   Alkmeon (I) son of Megakles (I) (first at Olympia, 592) :APF 9688, II.

2,3   Kallias (I) son of Phainippos (I) (first at Pythia in 570 or 566,
          second at Olympia 564) : APF 7826, II.

4   Miltiades (III) son of Kypselos (first at Olympia, 548?) : APF 8429,VI.

5   Alkmeonides (I) son of Alkmeon (I) (first at Panathenaia, 546) : APF
          9688, III.

6,[7],8   Kimon (I) son of Stesagoras (I) (first at Olympia, 536, [532], and
          528) : APF 8429, VII.

[7]   Peisistratos (II) son of Hippokrates (first at Olympia 532 by
          transference) : APF 11793.

9   Alkibiades (I) (first at Pythia, 525-500) : APF 600, V.

(-   Kallias (II) son of Hipponikos (I) of Alopeke (allegedly first at
          Olympia 500, 496, and 492 or 496, 492, and 484) : APF 7826, V.)

10   Descendant of Alkmeon (I) (first at Pythia before 486) : APF 9688, II.

11-15   Descendants of Alkmeon (I) (first at Isthmia five times before 486) :
          APF 9688, II.

16   Megakles (III) son of Hippokrates (I) of Alopeke (first at Pythia, 486):
          APF 9688, X.

17-19   Pronapes son of Pronapides of Prasiai (first at Nemea, Isthmia, and
          Panathenaia in the mid fifth century) : APF 12250.

20-22   Lysis (I) of Aixone and Demokrates (I) son of Lysis (I) of Aixone
          (first at Nemea, Isthmia, and Pythia in the fifth century, one or two

of these victories being in the two-horse contest) : APF 9574.

23   Megakles (V) son of Megakles (III) of Alopeke (first at Olympia, 436):
      APF 9688, XI.

24–33 Alkibiades (III) son of Kleinias (II) of Skambonidai (first at
       Panathenaia, 418?, first at Nemea and Pythia by 416, first, second,
       and fourth, and four other entries at Olympia, 416) : APF 600, IX.

[33]   Teisias (II) son of Teisimachos of Kephale (subverted entry
       at Olympia, 416) : APF 13479.

34,35 Lost Name 1 (first at Isthmia and Nemea before 390) : APF 5951.

36   Chabrias son of Ktesippos (I) of Aixone (first at Pythia, 374) :
       APF 15086.

37,38 [– –]los son of Promachos of Eleusis (first at Panathenaia and
       [Eleusinia?], both in the two-horse contest, before ca. 350) : APF
       12245.

39   Timokrates (II) son of Antiphon of Krioa (first at Olympia in the
       two-horse contest, 352?) :·APF 13772.

40   Demades (I) son of Demeas (I) of Paiania (first at Olympia, perhaps
       in the two-horse contest, 328?) : APF 3263.

41,42,43 Demetrios (I) son of Phanostratos of Phaleron (first at Panathenaia,
       Delia, and Hermaia ca. 320) : APF 3455.

44   Lost Name 21 (first at Ilieia in the two-horse contest, end of the
       fourth century) : APF D 21.

INDEX I

INDEX LOCORUM

Inscriptions

Literary Texts

INDEX II

Index of Subjects

absentee landlord 56 f, 60
adoption law, 73 f
administrative skills, importance of,
  115 f
agonistic liturgies, lists not kept
  for, 24 f
  numbers per year, 27
agricultural wealth, 38
alienability of land, 40
anchisteia, 74
antidosis, 9, 16, 26, 76, 83
aretē, 26
Aristophon, measures attributable
  to, 144 f
athletic prowess as basis of
  political position, 99
Attic Stelai, 47
autourgoi, 43 f
bankers, 65 ff
banking, 64 ff
bankruptcies, 79
bilateral kindred, 74
booty, 66 ff
bottomry loans, 60 ff
bribery, 66 ff
cavalrymen, vi 36
charis, 92 ff, 129
childlessness, 73
children, exposure of, 76
Chios, 46
choice within liturgical system, 26, 89,
  91 ff
citizens as bankers' agents, 65
conspicuous consumption, 84
costs of liturgies, 9, 82
cult power, 105 ff, 126
conspicuous consumption, 84
costs of liturgies, 9, 82
cult-power, 105 ff, 126
cult-properties liable to eisphora, 137
cults, regulation of, by the State,
  110 ff
demarchs, role in administration, 146 f
Demosthenes, reform of trierarchy, 12,
  19
Demotionidai, 105 ff
diadikasia, 9, 16, 83, 133 ff
diadikasia documents, 30, 33, 133 ff
diapsephismos, 107

eisphora, effects of incidence of,
  82 f
Eleusis, as cult-centre, 109
emotional detachment from land,
  75 f
endogamy, 76 f
epidoseis, 66, 91
  declining to contribute to, 89
eranos-loans, 62
euporoi 4, 10 ff
expenditure as basis of political
  position, 96 ff, 116 f, 129
family ability, decline in, 84 f
family political tradition, in
  sixth and fifth centuries,
  120 f
  lack of, in fourth century, 121
fragmentation of estates, 75
genē, loss of cult-power by, 112
genos as organic part of phratry,
  106
gentilician control of cults, 109 ff
Golden Age without slaves, motif of,
  in comedy, 47
goodwill of propertied class,
  need for, 90
grave monuments, 5
'Greater Demarchy' of Erchia, 108
hektemoroi, 55
hoarding, 39 with n.3
homonymity within a deme, 5
horse-rearing, 29, 31, 97 ff,
  101 ff, 167 f.
horses, prices of, 100n15
house-prices, 50
illustriousness, 100
imperialism, motives for, 60, 78,
  90
industrial slave-owning, 41 ff,
  69 f
interest rates, 64, 80
kaloskagathos, use of term, 71
klerouchies, 56
Korinth, 45
landed aristocracy, disappearance
  of, 71
land, normally the safest investment, 77 f.
land ownership outside Attika,
  55 ff, 58 ff, 78, 90

MONOGRAPHS
IN CLASSICAL STUDIES

Adler, Eve. **Catullan Self-Revelation.** 1981

Arnould, Dominique. **Guerre et Paix dans la Poesie Grecque.** 1981

Block, Elizabeth. **The Effects of Divine Manifestations on the Reader's Perspective in Vergil's** *Aeneid.* 1981

Bowie, Angus M. **The Poetic Dialect of Sappho and Alcaeus.** 1981

Brooks, Robert A. **Ennius and Roman Tragedy.** 1981.

Brumfield, Allaire Chandor. **The Attic Festivals of Demeter and Their Relation to the Agricultural Year.** 1981.

Carey, Chrstopher. **A Commentary on Five Odes of Pindar.** 1981

David, Ephraim. **Sparta Between Empire and Revolution (404-243 B.C.).** 1981

Davies, John K. **Wealth and the Power of Wealth in Classical Athens.** 1981

Doenges, Norman A. **The Letters of Themistokles.** 1981.

Figueira, Thomas J. **Aegina.** 1981.

Furley, William D. **Studies in the Use of Fire in Ancient Greek Religion.** 1981.

Ginsburg, Judith. **Tradition and Theme in the** *Annals* **of Tacitus.** 1981.

Hall, Jennifer. **Lucian's Satire.** 1981.

Hillyard, Brian P. **Plutarch:** *De Audiendo.* 1981

Hine, Harry M. **An Edition with Commentary of Seneca,** *Natural Questions,* **Book Two.** 1981

Horrocks, Geoffrey C. **Space and Time in Homer.** 1981

Lipovsky, James. **A Historiographical Study of Livy.** 1981

McCabe, Donald Francis. **The Prose-Rhythm of Demosthenes.** 1981

Parry, Adam Milman. *Logos* and *Ergon* in Thucydides. 1981

Patterson, Cynthia. **Pericles' Citizenship Law of 451-50 B.C.** 1981

Pernot, Laurent. **Les** *Discours Siciliens* **d'Aelius Aristide (Or. 5-6).** 1981

Philippides, Dia Mary L. **The Iambic Trimeter of Eruipedes.** 1981

Rash, James Nicholas. **Meter and Language in the Lyrics of the** *Suppliants* **of Aeschylus.** 1981

Skinner, Marilyn B. **Catullus'** *Passer.* 1981

Spofford, Edward W. **The Social Poetry of the Georgics.** 1981

Stone, Larua M. **Costume in Aristophanic Comedy.** 1981

Szegedy-Maszak, Andrew. **The** *Nomoi* **of Theophrastus.** 1981

Taylor, Michael W. **The Tyrant Slayers.** 1981

White, F.C. **Plato's Theory of Particulars.** 1981

Zetzel, James E.G. **Latin Textual Criticism in Antiquity.** 1981

Ziolkowski, John E. **Thucydides and the Tradition of Funeral Speeches at Athens.** 1981